This is the clearest and most comprehensive book I've ever read on what it means for a church to become a healthy parenting church. I'm praying that church leaders of every denomination will read this book, believe it, and prepare the church to enter into the parenting process. I enthusiastically recommend *The Ripple Church*.

Keith M. Wright
District Superintendent, Kansas City District
Church of the Nazarene

When I first met Phil Stevenson, my heart leapt. Here was a kindred spirit, a fellow planter, a visionary. This is not theory—this is lived-out, crucible-tested, battle-proven church multiplication teaching. If you want your church to make a broader impact on our world, I suggest you listen carefully, and then put it into practice.

Marcus Bigelow
President, Stadia: New Church Strategies

Phil Stevenson doesn't just talk church planting, he makes it happen—and his book tells us how to do it. The church teaches individuals the importance of generosity and multiplication while sometimes forgetting that the local church itself should also practice those same virtues. If only half of the local churches caught this idea (including "small" ones the size of most New Testament churches), we'd see a massive ingathering to God's kingdom. You'll like this practical "how to" book, but be careful—once you've read it, there will be no more excuses for not becoming a ripple church!

Keith Drury
Assistant Professor, Indiana Wesleyan University

Phil Stevenson gives us a plan for a successful church that is different: the focus is not only growing the local church but being resourceful in developing a movement to plant churches. The emphasis is on God's faithfulness to those who "risk obedience." This is not a "one formula fits all" approach but one that provides clarity in presenting valuable insights learned through experience.

Stephen F. Babby
District Superintendent, Pacific Southwest District
The Wesleyan Church

The ripple church principle is a fresh approach to church planting. I was captivated by the whole concept. Reading this book will stimulate purpose, direction, and growth in the hearts of church planters.

Stan Toler
senior pastor, author, and leader in church development

In *The Ripple Church*, we see Phil Stevenson at his best! Phil not only is one of North America's foremost experts who has studied and taught the parent church process, but he has practiced it for years in his own life and ministry.

Larry McKain
Executive Director, New Church Specialties

The Ripple Church

The Ripple Church

Phil Stevenson

wesleyan
publishing
house

Indianapolis, Indiana

Copyright © 2004 by The Wesleyan Church
Published by Wesleyan Publishing House
Indianapolis, Indiana 46250
Printed in the United States of America

ISBN 0-89827-271-8

Library of Congress Cataloging-in-Publication Data

Stevenson, Phil.
    The ripple church / Phil Stevenson.
       p. cm.—(The leading pastor series)
    Includes bibliographical references.
    ISBN 0-89827-271-8 (pbk.)
    1. Church development, New. I. Title. II. Series.
    BV652.24.S74 2004
    254'.1—dc22   2003027553

This book is dedicated to the courageous and committed people of Arcade Wesleyan Church who accepted the call to sacrificially and willingly invest themselves in the Kingdom through the parenting of new, reproducing churches.

CONTENTS

—⟋⟍⟋—

FOREWORD

—⟋⟍⟍⟍—

P hil Stevenson gets it. If we are going to penetrate our world
for Jesus, we must *multiply* our congregations while we *add*
converts to them.

The congregation Phil pastored in Sacramento has, in effect,
grown by 450 percent in just six years. All this has come through
the multiplication of churches. Phil and his team have not been
effective only at planting churches; they have gone the extra mile
by building reproducibility into the churches they have started. The
mother church is now credited with six daughter churches and three
granddaughter congregations.

This could happen to you. It will cost you something, but it
will add something as well. The costs are obvious. You give away
a few people. You invest some money. You experience the sadness
of seeing great friends move into a new worship situation. But the
benefits easily outweigh the costs. You get to be a vital part of the
expansion of the kingdom of God.

The Kingdom grows fastest when we start new churches
because newer congregations tend to grow much faster than older
ones. When your congregation parents a new church, your overall
growth accelerates, so Kingdom growth is obvious. Then there is
the multiplication factor. Each succeeding generation of new
churches has the ability to reproduce itself, so a whole movement
is born.

This has been my experience. Starting with just twelve people in
1971, my wife, Ruby, and I started a new church. That tiny congregation has now grown into more than two hundred congregations
spread around the world. I don't personally know most of the leaders.

Some of them, I will never meet in my life. The churches belong to Jesus. They make up his Kingdom, not mine.

This book could start you on an exciting journey. You may some-day find that you have started a movement, or even several of them. But remember, the book is not called "Six Easy Steps to Multiplication." Phil writes about letting the Spirit lead into new ter-ritory. He strongly expects each new church to be a unique creation.

As you read this book, I pray that the Holy Spirit will speak to your heart and that you will be able to imagine a new church in some area that is available to you. It may be just a few miles down the road. It may be in another country. My prayer is simply that you will get hold of the vision Phil has to plant wherever the Spirit leads.

—RALPH MOORE
Founding Pastor, Hope Chapel Kaneohe Bay
Author, *Starting A New Church*

ACKNOWLEDGEMENTS

—⁓⁓—

To Dr. Jerry Pence whose encouragement and editing was critical in bringing this book to reality.

To my wife, Joni, who kept me writing.

To the Wesleyan Publishing House editing team, led by Lawrence Wilson.

To the leaders who willingly started churches out of Arcade Wesleyan Church: Craig Evans of Eskaton Village Community Church; Pastor V. Ebenezar of Medak, India; Mark Welch of Spring Valley Church; Keith Klassen of Midtown Community; Brett Hilgemann of Lighthouse Fellowship; and Jim Bogear of The River Church.

To the granddaughter churches who have continued the ripple.

INTRODUCTION

———〜〜〜———

You've seen the image a thousand times. A rock is tossed into a pond. The rock makes a splash. Ripples emanate from the point of impact, spreading across the surface of the water until they reach the other shore. We call it the ripple effect.

In that same way, a new generation of churches is creating a ripple effect across the country. Led by men and women of vision, these congregations are extending their influence out from the center, into their communities and across their regions.

How?

A few courageous leaders have done what few in the twenty-first century church are willing to do. They have turned their focus outward, planting new churches rather than simply gathering more people into existing ones. These ripple churches have become points of impact for a movement that is spreading around the world.

But it hasn't been easy. By choosing influence over influx, ripple churches have sacrificed their own comfort and security in order to bring forth the next generation of Christians. They have abandoned contemporary notions of success in order to bring about Kingdom growth. They have been willing to swim against the stream of popular culture.

Is it worth it?

Nimbus Dam is located roughly fifteen miles east of downtown Sacramento, California, a short jaunt up the Highway 50 corridor toward the south shore of Lake Tahoe. Nimbus Dam controls the water flow of the American River as it makes its way west toward the Sacramento River and, ultimately, to the Pacific Ocean.

The river's current can be brisk, especially in the fall, when an extraordinary event occurs. That's when salmon make their way east from the ocean, swimming against the west-flowing current. The fish head upriver in order to spawn. The journey requires tremendous energy, and many salmon die along the way. But they complete this trip, swimming against the flow, in order to reproduce. If they don't, their species will not survive.

The salmon could, I suppose, live out their lives downstream. It would be more comfortable, with no current to fight and no risk. Upstream is unknown to them. To swim upstream demands an effort they may not be able to muster. Yet these creatures seem to know that something exists upstream that can be found nowhere else: the opportunity to create a new generation.

In fact, the salmon that make their way against the current each fall are themselves the product of a preceding generation's effort. Their predecessors expended the energy to swim against the tide so they could create new life. This year yet another generation of salmon will make that same journey. The cycle of growth continues.

Today, the church desperately needs a new generation of leaders that is willing to swim against the current. Too many of us enjoy the relative calm of downstream life. We convince ourselves that gathering more people around us in a single church will ensure the existence of the species. It won't. A large school of salmon swimming comfortably in the warm ocean will not survive indefinitely. Those salmon must fight their way upstream to create new life. Similarly, we must sacrifice our time, energy, and money if we are to create new congregations. The survival of the church depends upon it.

This will never be easy. In the current church culture, bigger is considered better. We measure ourselves by buildings, bodies, and budgets, and the bottom line is weekly worship attendance. In this climate, the idea of planting new churches out of existing ones raises a few eyebrows. Therefore leaders who participate in the church planting movement must swim against popular opinion. They must be willing to abandon commonly held notions about achievement and success. To stay downstream is much easier. Yet as Zig Ziglar noted, even a dead fish can swim downstream. The kind of multiplication that will ensure the future of the church can never happen in the downstream culture. We need to swim against the tide.

So the challenge for today's church leaders is twofold. First, we must realize the need to propagate the gospel by multiplying congregations, and then we must sacrifice in order to do so. That will mean resisting the temptation merely to grow larger as a congregation, and that will require faith.

We risk much by swimming upstream. It's always easier to stay where we are—complacent and comfortable. We need leaders who have the God-given faith to move forward in spite of fear and uncertainty. By doing so, we will lay the foundation for an entire new generation of believers. Lives will be transformed. The church will be revolutionized. The entire world will be changed.

Will you accept this challenge? Will you move beyond the small circle of your own comfort and begin the ripple that will affect your community and your world? I saw a television advertisement that touted its product this way: "It began with a drop that caused a ripple, which caused a wave, which caused the whole world to stand up and take notice." One drop does make a difference. One leader can begin a great movement. One ripple can change the world.

Will it begin with you?

CHAPTER ONE

HOW GOD MADE
A CHURCH PLANTER
OUT OF ME

—⁓—

> ### RIPPLE PRINCIPLE
> God enlarges his Kingdom by casting a
> vision for church planting.

I have always been intrigued by the call of Gideon. When God called Gideon, he was in a winepress, threshing wheat (see Judg. 6). In reality, Gideon was hiding from the Midianites, who had been raiding Israelite territory. Gideon wanted nothing to do with the Midianites, but God had other plans for this young man. It was God's plan that Gideon would defeat the mighty Midianite army with a force of only three hundred men using not weapons but clay pots and torches. Who could blame Gideon for hiding?

Of course, God didn't reveal the whole plan to Gideon at once. That would have been overwhelming. The first step was for Gideon to get out of the winepress—the place where he felt safe. Gideon didn't know all that God had in mind, but he had to be willing to let go of his security and step out of his familiar surroundings. He had to take a step of faith.

God is still calling people to accomplish great things. Often, these are people who are living—or hiding—in their comfort zone and have no desire to take on a challenge. They're people like Gideon, people like me.

This is the story of how God called me out of the winepress, which was my secure ministry at a comfortable church, and gave me a dream for reaching thousands of people with the gospel. It's a story that begins in a little Presbyterian church in the southeast section of San Diego.

EARLY EXPERIENCES

My first recollection of church is of the small congregation that my family attended when I was a child. My dad was an usher, my mom was the Sunday school superintendent, and they both led the young adult group. In those days it seemed that my family was always at church. My best buddies were the pastor's son and the music director's son, and we became something like the Three Musketeers. We had mastered the art of having fun and knew how to stand right on the edge of trouble without falling into it.

Every Sunday, my parents gave me a nickel to put in the offering. What they didn't know was that at the Rexall drug store not more than a block from the church, a nickel could purchase two bubble gum cigars. This made for an agonizing decision. I had one nickel and two places to invest. One Sunday a friend and I agreed that the bubble gum cigars made much more sense than the offering plate. So when Mom and Dad were taking care of their responsibilities, we headed to the corner store to take care of ours.

Everything would have worked out fine if we had been able to keep the cigars in our pockets during church. Since we were sitting in the back of the church, we figured no one would notice what we were doing and began to "smoke" our cigars. We really put on an act, emulating every cigar-chomping actor we had ever seen on television. There we were, in the middle of the church service, pretending to be in our own smoke-filled world. Just as we'd thought, none of the worshipers noticed us. But an usher did. Did I mention that my dad was an usher?

Within seconds there was a tap on my shoulder. There stood my dad, whose glaring look clearly told me to follow him outside. I won't go into details, but my dad "persuaded" us that cigar smoking in church would be a one-time event. Not surprisingly, I have never done so again, with bubble gum or otherwise!

I had many fun times at that Presbyterian church, so it came as a shock when my parents informed me that we would soon begin attending somewhere else: a Wesleyan church called Skyline. I knew the place. It was a huge building that we passed each week on the way to our church. My sister had been invited to attend the youth group, which was led by a crazy guy who went by the initials PJ, for Pastor Jimmy. Pastor Jimmy Johnson was, well, a little different. He drove around town in an old hearse, had a loud laugh, and knew how to get the attention of teenagers with creativity and innovation. Skyline was a very large church; over one thousand people attended its three Sunday morning services. Each week there was enthusiasm, excitement, and excellence. I loved every minute of it!

It was at Skyline that I heard a clear presentation of the gospel message. I became a Christian just before entering the seventh grade. In my senior year of high school, I sensed and accepted a call into full-time Christian service. Based on my experience of church so far, my mission seemed clear: to bring as many people as possible to a saving knowledge of Jesus. The result, I knew, would be even more people attending our already large youth group. I envisioned numerical growth, big programs, and lots of large-scale events. In my mind, success in ministry meant having more people attending than before.

By 1980 I had completed a master's degree with emphases on theology and philosophy. The degree sounded impressive, but probably made me sound smarter than I really was. Fortunately, I was offered a one-year internship at my home church, Skyline Wesleyan. It was an incredible opportunity, and the experience laid a priceless foundation for my ministry. The vision I caught, the lessons I learned, the dreams that were born in my heart, and the people I encountered were unforgettable.

During my intern year, I attended Robert Schuller's Institute for Successful Church Leadership. There I was energized by Schuller's story. The idea of starting a church at a drive-in theater captivated me, and the venture of faith that led Schuller to purchase land and build the Tower of Hope tugged at my imagination. Hearing those stories while sitting in the recently completed Crystal Cathedral fueled my vision. Schuller's example became another influence on my ministry journey. I was envisioning great things.

Near the end of my intern year, I began seeking a permanent ministry appointment. I felt a distinct call to youth ministry, yet I knew that youth ministry positions in my denomination were difficult to come by. Most churches were not large enough to hire staff pastors, and the churches that were had already filled their positions. As I sat before the ordination board for my final interview, I realized that I might have to switch denominations in order to pursue my ministry call. Then one of the board members made this bizarre suggestion: "Have you considered planting a church?"

"No."

That was easy enough. There was no way I would consider starting a new congregation. I didn't know much about ministry, but I had already observed that the methods used to plant new churches were recipes for disaster. Usually, it involved a drop kick. They would *drop* a church planter into a community and then *kick* him until he dug a congregation out of nothing. A few tenacious leaders had succeeded in producing new congregations under those conditions, but those pastors seemed to be the exception. I wanted no part of church planting.

My opportunity to serve as a full-time youth pastor came at First Church of the Nazarene in Atlanta, Georgia, where I came under the tutelage of Dr. Keith Wright. He taught me much about cultivating and maintaining relationships. Then, in 1982, I was invited to take my dream job: youth pastor at Skyline Wesleyan Church. I had great memories of my own youth at Skyline and high hopes for a successful ministry. As a bonus, Skyline was the largest church in its denomination, which provided instant recognition to my efforts. Dr. John Maxwell was the senior pastor at Skyline, and my tenure under his ministry became a graduate-level degree in leadership. In six years on his staff, I learned tremendous lessons on leadership principles. It was an incredible environment. I discovered not merely how to dream but how to develop dreams into reality. This was another critical phase in my ministry life.

By 1988 I had, I thought, achieved a great deal in ministry. I had worked with some of the most capable leaders in the evangelical church, and I had directed a youth ministry that influenced hundreds of young people every year. What I thought was the top, however, was just the beginning of my ministry journey.

A Vision Implanted

In 1988 God called my family and me to join the staff at Arcade Wesleyan Church in Sacramento, California. Dr. Karl Westfall was the senior pastor, and he had a tremendous vision for the church. Arcade had been a flagship church in its district for years. Over the previous decade, it had consistently averaged more than four hundred in worship attendance, and it had successfully planted two churches in the Greater Sacramento area. The church was built on youth, music, and solid pastoral leadership. It was a great opportunity, and I was happy to take it.

There was one problem at Arcade, however. The church's facility was landlocked. It's three hundred-seat sanctuary, educational wing, and office space occupied less than two acres of land, and there were only fifty-four parking spaces. Double parking was common, which led to some genuine tests of Christian love and patience when people were ready to leave church at different times!

In spite of the space problem, the church was thriving. There were multiple services, cars parked up and down the side streets, and the building teemed with people. Something significant was bubbling to the surface. Lives were being transformed, new Sunday school classes were beginning, and we were considering the use of off-site facilities to meet the demand for space. I knew that something big was happening in the church. What I didn't suspect was that God was also doing something big in me. That something began with a simple drive on the freeway.

THE I-80 VISION

Interstate 80 begins in Ridgefield Park, New Jersey, and passes through Sacramento, California, ending at the San Francisco Bay. Our little slice of this three-thousand-mile thoroughfare is known as the I-80 Corridor, a stretch of highway between Sacramento and San Francisco. It was on this freeway that God reached into my life and whispered a challenge that would radically transform my ministry.

I had been on staff at Arcade for about two years, and I was greatly enjoying my work there. Dr. Westfall gave me opportunities that most staff pastors would pay for. He allowed me to begin a Sunday school class for young families, which became an entry point into the church for many people. He gave me the responsibility to develop a leadership curriculum for the entire church and invited me to attend every board meeting. I was having a great time.

During those two years, I had traveled the I-80 Corridor many times and often took note of the number of new homes being built between Sacramento and San Francisco. Then one day, this thought occurred to me: *Someone ought to plant churches here.* I didn't take the idea personally. It just seemed reasonable that new churches ought to accompany the many new people moving into the area. *Yes,*

I though, *someone ought to take care of this*. Little did I realize that God was planting that dream in my own mind.

Over time, God refined my thought into a prayer, and the "someone" began to hit closer to home. *My denomination ought to plant churches here,* I thought. We didn't have many churches in northern California, and this would be an ideal place to expand. *Sure,* I thought, *my denomination could do this. We're an evangelistic group. Why hasn't anyone thought of this before?* During one of those drives along I-80, God whispered this challenge: *Why don't you do something about it?*

It was a genuine Moses moment. *Who, me?* I asked God. *No way. You must have forgotten whose prayer you were responding to. I have no experience at church planting. I don't know how to do it. I don't even like the idea. You definitely have the wrong guy.*

Strangely, God was silent after my outburst. That left me to brood upon the challenge that he had whispered into my mind. In time, I realized God really was calling me to plant a church. It didn't make any sense, but what else could I conclude? I told Joni, my wife, what I was thinking and we prayed about it together. Finally, we agreed that we would pursue this possibility.

Soon Joni and I began looking for a place to start a church. Fairfield is a beautiful city halfway between Sacramento and the Bay Area. *Why not split the difference?* we thought. Joni and I took exploratory trips to Fairfield and found a spot where many new homes were being built and a new school had just been completed. This would be the place. After several months of prayer and exploration, we were willing to step out in faith and begin a new congregation.

Then came another whisper. *You will not be the church planter,* the Lord said, *but you will help plant many churches through existing ones.*

Huh?

What on earth could that mean? Perhaps it was better that I didn't know.

THE RIPPLE PRINCIPLE UNFOLDS

After I said yes to the idea of planting a new church in Fairfield, God began to reveal a larger dream. My willingness to become a church planter was an act of faith; it was stepping out of the winepress to follow God. Once I had done that, God began to show me what might happen if a church—not just a single church planter—began to plant churches. What if the Arcade church did that? We could plant congregations to the north, south, east, and west. Each of those new churches would then plant churches, which would in turn plant even more churches. In time, a single congregation could be responsible for the birth of new churches as far away as San Francisco to the west, Reno to the east, Bakersfield to the south, and Redding to the north.

Immediately, an image formed in my mind. I envisioned someone taking a rock and throwing it into a pond. The rock made a tremendous impact where it landed, and ripples emanated from that point outward, eventually reaching to every shore. That one rock had changed the surface of the entire pond. I quickly sketched this vision on a piece of yellow paper. First I drew a circle, the point of impact, and labeled it "Arcade Wesleyan Church." Then I drew arrows leading out in four directions and labeled each with the name of a destination city.

There it was, the master plan!

So what did I do with this dream? I put it away. I took the yellow piece of paper, placed it in a file, and put it in a drawer. I was not the senior pastor of Arcade, and it was not my role to lead the congregation. My responsibility was to help my senior pastor fulfill his God-given dream, which, at that time, did not include parenting new churches. It would be three long years before I would return to that yellow paper and the dream it represented.

THE RIGHT TIME

In 1991 God called Joni and me to lead a congregation in Southern California, where I followed a long-term and highly regarded pastor. God graciously provided wisdom, and we saw consistent growth. When the church expanded its facilities, I learned how to lead change in a congregation. I thought of myself as gaining valuable experience as a senior pastor. I had no idea that God was still preparing me to act on the dream of multiplying congregations.

One morning in 1994, I was in my office early when the private phone rang. I knew it would be Joni. "You just got a call from Jeff Jennings," she said. "He will be calling you in a few minutes, and I wanted to make sure you answer the phone."

Jeff was a leader in the Arcade Wesleyan Church and a good friend. I had the privilege of being his discipleship partner while at Arcade. I knew that Pastor Westfall had just resigned, and Arcade was beginning the search for a new pastor. Honestly, I hoped he was calling about the position. Realistically, I assumed he was calling to get names of potential candidates. But when the phone rang a minute or two later, the first words out of Jeff's mouth were these: "Are you ready to come back to Sacramento?"

I was excited and cautious at the same time. Jeff and I talked about the past three years, and we both had lots of questions. I wanted to know the atmosphere of the church. Why was the pastor leaving? Did the church want to move in a new direction?

Secretly, I was excited about the possibility. My family loved northern California, and my vision for the area was still crystal clear. I knew it was early in the search process, but my attitude was, *God, unless you have a real problem with this, I'd like to go back!*

As we ended the conversation, Jeff said he would get back to me in a few days. I hung up the phone and walked straight to my filing cabinet. I opened the top drawer and pulled out a yellow piece of paper with a rough-drawn diagram—a circle and four arrows. I read the names of the four destination cities, and the image of the rippling pond flooded back to my mind. I held the paper up to God and said simply, "Lord, if it's time, I'm ready."

A DREAM NOT A WISH

We returned to Sacramento in September 1994. The entire family was thrilled to be back, and I was eager to get to work. I had a dream, one that was imbedded in the fabric of my being. Parenting churches was not something I wanted to do; it was something I *had* to do. Yet my entire plan was that rough sketch on yellow notebook paper. I knew that I needed a more definite strategy if the dream was to become reality.

ASSESSMENT

My first step was to assess the present situation of the church. I needed to know where Arcade was before I could lead it to where I thought it should be. I met with people of influence in the church. I observed. I asked questions. But I made no attempt to initiate change. During that time I identified several internal needs that had to be addressed. They were not serious, but they were potential roadblocks to moving forward with the dream of parenting churches.

One problem was that the building needed maintenance. Since the congregation had thought seriously about relocating, it had not invested adequately in the facility. If we were to stay here, some improvements would be needed. In order to send people out—parenting new churches—we would also need to attract new people in, and our deteriorating facility was an obstacle to returning guests. We put together a team to plan renovations.

LEARNING

The second step was to refine the ripple principle that I had sketched on yellow paper more than three years earlier. I began to share with the congregation the future I sensed God intended for us. Arcade was going to be a growing church. It was going to make an impact in its community. Beyond that, it would be the rock in the pond of Sacramento. We would ripple throughout the Greater

Sacramento Area by planting churches that would in turn plant churches. And that would be just the beginning. I shared my dream to see churches in Redding, Bakersfield, and Reno as a result of Arcade's willingness to look beyond itself. I cast a general vision, for that was all I had.

At the same time, I examined every resource on church planting I could find. I learned a great deal, and shared as much as I could with my staff. A key book for my leadership team was C. Peter Wagner's *Church Planting for a Greater Harvest*. I purchased copies and put them into the hands of my leaders. Another critical book was *Let Go of the Ring* by Ralph Moore. Ralph had led congregations that had planted over two hundred daughter churches. I also learned much from Wayne Schmidt, pastor of Kentwood Community Church near Grand Rapids, Michigan. Kentwood has continued to grow while parenting new churches, and Wayne shared insights that became instrumental in Arcade's parenting effort. One revelation was what I call *the Gut Principle*. As Wayne put it, "You can do all the research and demographics you want when deciding where to plant a church. But never underestimate your gut. Where do you sense you need to begin?"

As I learned from these leaders, a strategic plan began to emerge. Unrelated strands were knitted together into a strong cord, and the Arcade church was beginning to own the idea of creating a ripple across northern California.

SURVEY CHURCH PLANTERS

The third step was to survey church planters. This was not a scientific survey but more of a fact-finding venture. I sought out both leaders who had succeeded in planting new congregations and those who had crashed and burned. I asked one question: What were the biggest obstacles you faced? I received three consistent responses: loneliness, lack of finances, and difficulty in finding core team leaders. I knew that if Arcade could avoid those three roadblocks, our chance of success in parenting new churches would be much higher. I also knew that each of those barriers represented something that an established church could provide. Churches planting churches could make a difference.

After assessing the situation, learning as much as we could, and surveying a host of church planters, the Arcade church formed a plan to parent four reproducing churches by 2005. Our parenting cycle would begin in June 1997. Even I was amazed by the scope of this plan. Yet when we stepped out and let God step in, He exploded our dream to outrageous proportions.

RENOVATING PROPERTY AND PEOPLE

The renovation of Arcade's property provided a tangible starting point for change. The church rallied to the project. We raised a good deal of money and had workdays filled with so much laughter that they seemed more like a party with cake and ice cream than a project with hammers and crowbars. But I soon discovered that if we were to successfully parent a church, we would need a renovation of our hearts, not just our facility. That renovation came through the discovery of Henry Blackaby's book, *Experiencing God*.

As our leadership team studied the book together, we discovered the reality of Gal. 5:25: "Since we live by the Spirit, let us keep in step with the Spirit." We learned to allow God to direct our decision making. As we met together, we talked, sang, listened, and genuinely opened ourselves to God. We learned that the Spirit, not the strategy, must dictate the timing of any ministry venture.

I am a goal-oriented person, so when we declared that we would plant four churches by 2005, I thought the project would boil down to creating a timeline, assigning tasks, and getting the work done. That's how we began, but it's not how we ended.

I was determined to find our first church planter right away. I wrote a ministry description, placed an ad in our denominational magazine, made some phone calls, and followed up on leads. These are the things I thought would make the dream a reality. Then, when I encountered one dead end after another, I became anxious. We had a timeline. We had deadlines to meet. I had announced we were going to do this. What would happen to *my* credibility if we failed?

The situation came to a head at a staff meeting, where I bemoaned our inability to find a planter. That's when Laurie Jennings, one of our staff members, lobbed a shot right between my eyes. "We're not ready to plant a church," she said flatly.

I leveled my best senior-pastor look at her, the one that says, "Maybe you need to reconsider what you are saying." But she continued: "We're not healthy enough to plant a church. If we send out a core group from this church when we're in this condition, we'll plant a paraplegic church."

Deep down, I knew she was right. Still, it wasn't easy to hear. After all, as the pastor, the spiritual health of the congregation was my responsibility. Improving the health of this church could not be delegated. God used Laurie's words to force me to step back and listen more intently to him. *Don't you believe that I can plant four churches in four months if I choose?* the Lord asked. *Your plan may seem bold, but it's nothing compared to what I would like to do. You work on preparing the people spiritually and financially. When I think you're ready, I will provide you a planter.*

After that, we backed off our efforts to find a church planter and concentrated on preparation. We kept the goal of church planting before the people, but we avoided pointing toward dates and deadlines. Instead, we pointed to what God was doing in us and what he was saying to us. We discovered that God could do more in a minute than we could do in a year.

When we respond to God instead of reaching for goals, miraculous things happen. That is not to say that planning doesn't matter. It is a recognition of the fact that it is God, not our plans and goals, that directs us. God implants dreams in our hearts and minds. He gives us gifts and talents to carry out those dreams. Yet the dreams belong to him. When we become possessive of our God-given dreams, we may neglect the God who gave them. We must cherish the dream, but love the God who gave it even more.

FROM ADDITION TO MULTIPLICATION

Arcade's original plan to parent four reproducing churches by 2005 turned out to be shortsighted. The goal seemed huge to us at the time, and even if we had limited ourselves to our own plans and strategies, it would have been a masterful accomplishment. But God wanted more. We did eventually find a church planter, then another and another. So far, Arcade has parented six churches, which have produced three granddaughter churches. Each plant has been different in style and has used a different parenting model. God's creativity is incredible! He multiplies while we add.

Arcade's daughter churches, including two previous efforts, are—

- Riverside Wesleyan Church, Sacramento, Cal. (1969)

- East Roseville Parkway Bible Church, Roseville, Cal. (1984)

- Eskaton Village Community Church, Carmichael, Cal. (1996)

- Christian Believers Assembly, Medak, India (1997)

- Spring Valley Church, Rocklin, Cal. (Spring 1998)

- Midtown Community Church, Sacramento, Cal. (Summer 1998)

- Lighthouse Ministries, Elk Grove, Cal. (1999)

- The River Church, Sacramento, Cal. (2000)

Arcade's granddaughter churches are—

- Valley View Church, Lincoln, Cal. (1999)

- Sunday River Church, Rocklin, Cal. (2000)

- BridgePointe Church, El Dorado Hills, Cal. (2003)

By 2003 there were more than 1,800 people worshiping in Arcade and its daughter churches each Sunday, yet the Arcade church itself has never averaged more than 484 in worship attendance. Most of the new people would never have been reached if this courageous congregation had not been willing to break the ministry-influx mentality, the notion that it has to happen on our property if it is to count. Communities are being touched that the Arcade church would have never been able to infiltrate. As a result, the Kingdom is expanding.

This has been the impact of one congregation that caught a vision to go beyond itself. It swam against the current of the traditional church growth mentality, selflessly, sacrificially, and strategically moving into uncharted waters.

Destroy the Mold

I believe church planting is God's plan for expanding the Kingdom. Parenting reproducing churches is also the best solution to the ministry challenges of the twenty-first century. The diversity of our world demands it. Our world has too many needs, too many philosophies, and too many lifestyles for a single church to effectively minister to everyone.

Years ago some missionaries took the gospel to unreached cultures and tried to Americanize them at the same time. Although it seems silly now, these well-meaning evangelists did not consider their task complete until native believers wore shirts, pants, and shoes. Today's church is guilty of that same paternalism when it attempts to minister using cookie-cutter methods. An approach that works well in one environment may not be effective in other communities or with other people groups. By parenting churches, we begin unique ministries that are designed to meet specific needs of a particular community.

We must reject the model of success that simply measures the number of people gathered in one place. Genuine success is when men and women fulfill their God-given vision by creating new churches where there were none before. Established churches can make that happen by parenting reproducing congregations. We need all kinds of churches to parent all kinds of churches to reach all kinds of people using all kinds of models. It's time to break the mold and free the church to expand in every direction.

Has God given you that vision? Can you imagine the goal of churches planting churches? Can you see the ripple effect that your congregation might have on its community, its state, and its region? If God made a church planter out of me—the one-time youth pastor who flatly rejected the idea of starting a new congregation—he can do the same for you. It's time to step out of the winepress and accept the challenge of reaching our world. Accept the challenge. Make the wave that will cover your world.

CHAPTER TWO

THE BIBLICAL ROOTS
OF CHURCH PARENTING

—〰—

> **RIPPLE PRINCIPLE**
> Church planting has been God's plan
> from the beginning.

I have been a fan of college football coach Lou Holtz for years. He's had an amazing career. Holtz led Notre Dame to a national championship in 1988; he has coached four different college teams to top-twenty national rankings, and has won 238 regular season games and twelve bowl games. In 2001 he engineered the turnaround of the University of South Carolina football program, leading a team that was winless just two years before to a postseason bowl victory. In forty-three years of coaching, Lou Holtz has consistently demonstrated the ability to produce champions.

What's his secret?

In his book *Winning Every Day,* Holtz reveals one key for success. When making choices, he suggests, remember the letters W-I-N, which stand for *What's important now?*[1] Asking that simple question helps to determine priorities. It ensures that you concentrate on first things first. Take it from me, that works!

I believe churches need to ask that same question—What's important now? There are so many things we could be doing, but what *should* we be doing? What is the first priority? What is most important for the church of Jesus Christ right now?

The answer today is the same as it was when Jesus walked on this earth. Just before he ascended into heaven, Jesus gave the church its marching orders. He identified the W-I-N priority for us when he said plainly, "Go and make disciples . . ." (Matt. 28:19). The church is still in the disciple-making business. That has not changed, and until Christ returns, it never will. It's time to stop wringing our hands, wondering what we should be doing. We need to halt the endless meetings in which we discuss our purpose. Our mission is clear: *to go make disciples!* The most effective way of doing that, and the one we see modeled in the New Testament, is to create new congregations. That may be done by *church planting,* which is the establishment of an entirely new congregation, or by *church parenting,* the creation of a new church out of an existing one.

BACK TO BASICS

To evaluate the vitality of a business, consultants often ask two questions: What is your business? and How is business? The answers always reveal the state of the company's health. Two similar questions zero in on the condition of the church. Are we going? and Are we making disciples?

First, are we going? Is there a sending environment in the church today? What are we doing to create a sending atmosphere? Are we mobilizing people to infiltrate their culture, or do we have a come-to-us attitude? To go means to take Christ into our communities. It requires that we identify our spheres of influence and spread the gospel within them. Every believer influences some people; that's a given. What is less certain is our willingness to use that influence to imbue others with the presence of Jesus.

Second, are we making disciples? What are we doing to produce believers in Jesus Christ and cultivate faith within them? Our mission is not only to win people to Christ but also to wean them from the world. Disciple making is a long, arduous task. It involves meeting people where they are spiritually and moving them to where they need to be. It is relational, sometimes messy, but always meaningful.

Sadly, many churches would rather trade the difficult task of dealing with people for the easier task of developing programs. We prefer the quick-fix approach to making disciples that programs seem to offer. A new idea, a creative method, or a nicely packaged worship service may offer a short-term solution, but it will never fill the deep void in people's lives. Only a relationship with Christ can do that.

Several years ago I had a severe gall bladder attack and needed to have my gall bladder removed. During my hospital stay, a nurse offered me the painkiller Demerol. She asked, "Would you like it as a shot in your hip or through your IV?"

"What's the difference?" I asked.

She explained that injecting the drug through the IV would provide instant relief while the hip shot would take several minutes to kick in. At the time, my body needed instant relief. "Give me the IV," I said, and she shot the painkiller into the intravenous tube. The drug entered my bloodstream immediately, and the result was awesome. A warm feeling began at the bottom of my feet and rushed through my body. The pain was alleviated, and I was happy. For the next day or so, I looked forward to the nurse's visit every four hours. Those injections brought immediate relief.

But they didn't bring healing. What my body really needed was to mend, to be made whole again. It would have been shortsighted and unhealthy to depend only on the shots. They made me feel better, but they didn't make me well.

In the same way, it is shortsighted and unhealthy to rely only on programs to treat the needs of the church. We need to make and mature disciples of Christ; and to do that, we must go beyond where we are now. We need to accomplish more than what we can do in one place at one time. We must go out to engage our culture with the gospel.

Ripple churches understand the "Go and Make" mission. They have made the choice to go beyond themselves, reaching the lost by planting or parenting multiplying churches. Ripple churches release people to go, and going is necessary for making disciples. That has been God's plan from the beginning.

BEFORE IT WAS POPULAR

When I am around other pastors, it doesn't take long to get on the topic of planting churches. At one pastors' prayer meeting, a colleague mentioned that he had once planted a church. I was enthusiastic. "Then you know how important this is," I said eagerly. "You understand what I'm talking about."

I expected a wonderful, insightful exchange of ideas. What I received was a dour response. "Yes," the pastor said sourly. "I planted a church before it was popular." His tone suggested that church planting was simply another fad in the life of the church, a flavor-of-the-month program that would soon fade away. I couldn't resist a response.

"Church planting was pretty popular in the New Testament" I offered.

My friend didn't skip a beat. "Well, it wasn't *that* long ago," he joked.

His attitude is typical. Many church leaders view the renewed interest in planting as just another program. It is seen as this decade's church growth strategy, a mere fad. If that were true, then church planting would be optional. If you chose to do it, great! If not, there would be plenty of other programs to try.

Church planting, however, is not a whim or fashion. This strategy is firmly rooted in Scripture. In fact, church planting was the means God used to expand the New Testament church. Early disciples could not both go and stay at the same time. They could not both huddle in Jerusalem and hurl themselves into the expansion of the kingdom of

God. Those early disciples were on a mission. They had their marching orders, received on the Mount of Ascension: "Therefore, go and make disciples of all nations, baptizing them in the name of the Father and of the Son and of the Holy Spirit" (Matt. 28:19). Winning people to Christ and establishing churches to mature those new believers was the best way to carry out that mandate. It still is.

We cannot be a biblical church and abstain from planting churches. God never intended that the church should be just for us. His aim has always been to multiply the church, gathering more and more people to himself. Church planting is not about us, nor is it for us. It is for God. The goal is to gather more people to him.

Church planting is not the wave of the present; it is the wave of the past. However, this wave must break on the beaches of the twenty-first century. This ancient method must be applied in new ways for a new time. That will require our best energy. We need to rekindle the spirit of the Antioch church, a church that was so consumed with going and making that it released its best and the brightest to carry out the task (see Acts 13:1–3).

Paul and Barnabas were shining stars in the Antioch church. They must have contributed a great deal to the effectiveness of that congregation, so I'm sure it was difficult for the church to let them go. Keeping Paul and Barnabas in Antioch probably would have helped that one church grow, but the Kingdom would not have expanded as quickly as it did. By commissioning the two to go and plant new churches, the Antioch church not only continued to impact its community but also sent a ripple across the ancient world. In the mathematics of the Kingdom, subtraction often results in multiplication.

Paul understood that when he wrote to the church at Corinth, "Neither do we go beyond our limits by boasting of work done by others. Our hope is that, as *your faith continues to grow,* our area of activity among you will greatly expand, so that we can preach the gospel in the *regions beyond you*" (2 Cor. 10:15–16, emphasis added).

Paul had helped to establish the church in Corinth. It was the product of Antioch's sacrifice. To keep the vision for growth alive, Paul reminded the Corinthian Christians that the gospel now must be extended to the regions beyond them. How would that be accomplished? Paul told his Corinthian readers how it would happen: "As your faith continues to grow."

There are two critical requirements for fulfilling the biblical mandate to plant churches: mature faith and expanded vision. Both must be present if the gospel is to be spread. Mature Christians know that church is never just about us. Our faith must produce faith in others. And when our vision is expanded, the church will move into unknown regions. Our faith moves us beyond the seen to the yet-to-be seen. That's the way God has chosen to expand his Kingdom.

In Acts: Four Spheres of Influence

The book of Acts chronicles the beginnings of the church planting movement. In those days, multiplication was coded into the DNA of new congregations. Churches in the book of Acts wanted to impact a region, not just a single community. These churches never had the idea of becoming *regional churches* where people came from all over to worship in one spot. They wanted to be *regional ministries* that went out to make an impact over a broad area.

In Acts 1:8, Jesus promised, "You will receive power when the Holy Spirit comes upon you and you will be my witnesses in Jerusalem, and in all Judea and Samaria, and the ends of the earth." With that statement, Jesus identified four spheres of influence for the church. But he did not identify a single model for penetrating those spheres. Each local church must develop its own way of fleshing out this commission in order to reach each of its spheres.

Sphere One: Jerusalem

Jerusalem represents the people whom members of a congregation influence directly. Every believer knows someone who doesn't know Jesus. Three questions can help any believer identify those people in his or her Jerusalem. What do you do? Where do you do that? With whom do you do that? Those identified as the "whom" are in the sphere of influence.

SPHERE TWO: JUDEA

Judea is the geographic area surrounding a local church. The size of this area will vary. Churches in densely populated metropolitan areas may define their community as a half-mile radius surrounding their facilities. Rural churches may define their community as a town, or several towns, or perhaps the entire county. Each local church must identify and understand the character of its own Judea. Doing so is the first step to identifying practical methods for reaching that community.

SPHERE THREE: SAMARIA

Samaria is the sphere comprising those who are not apt to attend a particular local church because of distance, language or cultural difference, socioeconomic factors, life stage, style of ministry, or attitude. This includes people whose minds are closed to the church as a result of a previous bad experience or a misunderstanding of the institutional church. Samaria is best reached through the parenting of new reproducing churches. Reproducing churches are started with the expectation that they, too, will parent new churches. These new churches can be targeted at a specific group of people and be free to perform the ministries that will reach that group.

SPHERE FOUR: THE ENDS OF THE EARTH

Finally, the entire world is the object of each church's mission. Every congregation should include evangelistic strategies that involve its people in missionary endeavors around the globe.

Churches that are serious about obeying the Great Commission should address each of these four spheres of influence. Many churches are imbalanced, operating in only one or two spheres. It's up to local church leaders to ensure balance by leading their congregations to address each of the four.

Church planting began with the early church. It is time to once again involve local churches in such a movement. This mission cannot be left to just a few congregations, nor can we leave it to denominational officials. Existing churches in every place, of every size, and in all circumstances need to participate. The need is great. Many lost people are waiting for us to infiltrate their region with a message they can understand and in a way that attracts them to Christ.

ACROSS THE REGION

Many church leaders today want to develop regional churches, which gather people from a broad region to worship in a single place. These leaders expect to attract people from the surrounding communities to attend their churches, and they often do. People will drive some distance to the church's primary ministry facility. The philosophy of these churches is *ministry by influx*. The leaders ask, "How many people can we gather at one place at one time?"

A regional ministry is built on a different philosophy, *ministry by influence*. Leaders of regional ministries ask, "Whom are we influencing with the gospel?" Their goal is to provide diverse ministries to reach diverse peoples, and they plant various kinds of churches in order to achieve that goal.

Not every church can be a regional church, but every church can have a regional ministry, extending its influence over a broad area. By helping to multiply churches, every congregation can extend its influence throughout its region. Applebee's Neighborhood Grill and Bar, a well-known restaurant chain, provides a business analogy to regional ministry.

Consider Applebee's formula for growth, which it calls *conscious cannibalization*. Most restaurant chains carefully space their stores so that the sales of one don't eat into the sales of another. But Applebee's floods a territory with stores in order to gain brand recognition and market dominance. When most chains were building bigger and bigger restaurants, Applebee's designed smaller units, which were cheaper and faster to build, and easier to fill on slow days.[2]

It is possible for churches to adopt a similar regional mentality, which promotes the success of several locations, not just one or two. The question for church leaders is, Do you want a regional church or regional ministry? Are you interested in creating one successful church that gathers people from a broad region, or would you like to see many churches thriving throughout a given area?

OUT FROM THE CENTER

I have lived in California most of my life, a great deal of it in Southern California. California is well known for its Hollywood glitter, wonderful weather, trendsetting fashions, and eccentric celebrities. But nothing gets more attention from non-native Californians than an earthquake. In my out-of-state travels, the one question I can count on is "Have you ever been in an earthquake?" When I say yes, the follow-up is predictable: "What's it like?"

There are two kinds of earthquakes. One is the sudden jar, and it's something like a sonic boom. Windows rattle, houses shake, and before you realize what's happening, it's over. The other type of earthquake creates a rolling sensation in which the earth moves under you like an ocean swell. When that happens, the ground feels like a wave of soil. When it's over, you feel as if you have surfed an ocean breaker. Earthquakes come in different types, but all have something in common: an epicenter. The epicenter is the location of the quake's origin; it is where all the activity begins. All the energy—whether it's a big boom or a rolling wave—flows from the epicenter.

Like an earthquake, church planting may happen in various ways, but all emanate from an epicenter: the local church. The energy in church planting does not flow from denominational headquarters, departments of evangelism, seminaries, parachurch organizations or any other source. It flows from the local church. Existing churches exude the energy, creativity, and impetus needed to infiltrate the world. Denominations and parachurch organizations can support congregations in reproducing, but that role will be limited. The vision and determination to parent new congregations must come from the local church.

For too long, local churches have ignored their responsibility to reproduce. Resisting this critical aspect of their mission, most congregations have forced denominational organizations to take up the task of planting churches. Part of the reason is that individual Christians, too, have ignored their responsibility to evangelize. In an ideal world, believers produce believers, churches produce churches, and districts produce districts. But when believers stop reproducing themselves, churches try to do direct evangelism. That distracts churches from the task of producing new congregations. Districts and denominations are then drawn into the business of planting churches. The breakdown in personal evangelism has repercussions for church growth at every level.

It's time to change that. It's time for believers to spread the gospel by personal evangelism, and it's time for the local church to stop growing larger at the expense of Kingdom growth. It's time to return to our biblical roots and spread the gospel by multiplying congregations. Local churches must include parenting new churches as an integral part of their evangelism plan, and denominations should applaud and reward local churches that have the courage to reclaim their true mission.

Spreading the gospel by participating in the parenting of multiplying congregations is not new, nor is it optional for a Bible-believing, evangelistic congregation. It is the approach modeled in Scripture, and there simply is no other way to meet the great needs of a desperate world.

This is God's plan; this is our mission.

CHAPTER THREE

THE MOST EFFECTIVE FORM OF EVANGELISM

—⁓—

> ## RIPPLE PRINCIPLE
> New churches reach more people for Christ.

In his book *Church Planting for a Greater Harvest*, C. Peter Wagner declares boldly, "The single most effective evangelistic methodology under heaven is planting new churches."[1] That statement always elicits a strong reaction. Whenever I share this idea with a group of pastors, I can count on immediate feedback. Some will ask, "Does that mean that if I don't participate in planting churches, I'm not doing effective evangelism?" Others retort, "I don't agree with that. We are reaching many people for Christ, and we don't plant churches."

Once people get over the shock, however, I am able to point out that Dr. Wagner does not propose that church planting is the *only* viable evangelistic methodology but that it is the *most effective* one. If Wagner is correct, then every evangelistic church should want to participate in this movement. Effective churches employ every means they can to reach the world for Christ. Church planting must be a part of a full-orbed approach to evangelism.

WHY IT WORKS

The Church Multiplication Training Center reports the following statistics on the average number of converts produced by churches each year, per one hundred members.[2]

- Churches 0–3 years old: 10
- Churches 3–15 years old: 5
- Churches above 15 years old: 1.5

Obviously, new churches do a better job of bringing people to Christ. Lyle Schaller adds this insight:

> Planting new churches is the closest we have to a guaranteed means of reaching more people with the Good News that Jesus Christ is Lord and Savior. The historical record is clear that we cannot rely on long-established congregations to reach all the new generations of people.[3]

Why are new churches so effectively reaching the lost, disenfranchised, and unchurched? There are several reasons.

ATTRACTION

When I was a kid, I spent many hot summer evenings out on the front porch, the coolest spot in the house. I remember seeing all kinds of moths and other insects milling around the porch light. They were attracted to its light and warmth.

People are always attracted to the energy and vitality of a new venture. A Mexican restaurant opened recently in our area, and we decided to try it. We arrived for an early dinner at about 5:30 p.m., a time when there is typically no waiting line at local restaurants. We were surprised to find that there was already a twenty-minute wait for a table. That restaurant was not the only one offering Mexican cuisine that evening, but it was the latest. Most diners were there for the same reason: they wanted to try something new.

That's one reason that a new church is more likely to catch the attention of seekers and others who are looking for a church experience. Some people feel the need to attend church but put it off because they view existing churches as too rigid or difficult to break into. Parenting a new church provides a fresh opportunity for people to get plugged in. There are unchurched people who pass by your church every week, some of whom are looking for something new. You can offer it to them. Parenting a new church provides entry points for those who have found reasons to stay away from established congregations.

I once had the opportunity to preach at the opening service of a church in Southern California. After the service, I met a single mom who held in her hand one of the flyers that had been sent out by mail. When I asked why she decided to come to church, she said, "I just moved to the area, and I wanted to get my kids into church. When this flyer came in the mail, I thought this might be a good time to start." New things attract new people.

CAMARADERIE

Bonds between people are more easily formed in a church that is just beginning. Everyone is new, so it's easier for people to form relationships. People who have never attended church, or have not attended in quite some time, know that they will not be alone. They won't have to break into existing friendships and group structures.

Something similar happens when you move into a new home. There is a huge difference between moving into an established neighborhood and moving into a new one. I have done both, and it is far easier to establish friendships with neighbors in a new development. Everyone who lives there is a newcomer, and that forms a common bond. The same is true in a new church. Everyone enters together.

URGENCY

Another reason new churches are more effective at evangelism is that they have to be. Most existing churches would be fine, at least for awhile, if no new people were reached. Established churches have a solid core and can meet their budget with the existing group. That self-sufficiency can result in complacency. Before long, they may make only token efforts to reach outsiders.

A new church, on the other hand, must grow in order to survive. Its future depends on an influx of new people who are learning stewardship, deepening their faith, and developing their leadership abilities. Without a stream of new believers, the new church will die in its early stages.

FOCUS

New churches are on the cutting edge of the church's purpose—winning the lost to Christ. They are not preoccupied with maintenance because they have nothing to maintain. They want to move out and gain new territory. Not content with holding the beachhead, they want to take the entire island.

A man walked into a Circle K Store in Louisiana, placed a twenty-dollar bill on the counter, and asked for change. When the clerk opened the cash drawer, the man pulled a gun and demanded all the cash. The cashier complied with the gunman's demand, and rightly so. The robber took the cash and fled. In his haste, however, the gunman left the original twenty-dollar bill on the counter. So how much did he get from the cash drawer? Fifteen dollars. It actually cost the man five dollars to rob the store!

Too many churches are leaving the twenty on the counter. They have lost sight of their original purpose and are actually shrinking, in Kingdom terms, rather than growing. New churches seldom lose sight of their purpose. They're focused on reaching the lost for Christ.

FLEXIBILITY

New churches are flexible; they change more readily than existing churches. They do not live under the prohibitions of the past. In an established church, the familiar words "We've never done that before" often become a roadblock to change. In a new church, "We've never done that before" is an invitation to try. New churches are like speedboats; established churches are like supertankers. Having a speedboat mentality allows new congregations to make adjustments or change direction with little effort. They're usually willing to do whatever it takes to reach people for Christ.

BridgePointe Church was started in January 2003 in El Dorado Hills, California. This congregation began its ministry in an elementary school. A few months after the opening service, the opportunity to relocate to an abandoned real estate complex presented itself. Although the facility would need some work, it gave them a facility they could use twenty-four hours a day.

The church quickly decided to move and mobilized itself to complete the work. Because BridgePointe was a new congregation, there were few hoops through which to jump. The organizational structure was flexible enough to accommodate a quick change.

SPECIFICITY

New churches are effective at evangelism because they can afford to target the specific needs of people groups. New congregations don't have a host of stakeholders, each with an agenda; and they don't have to expend energy maintaining existing programs. Instead, new churches are free to aim their ministry at anyone they choose. They can focus on doing a few things well rather than doing many things with mediocrity.

Cascade Hills is a church plant in Redmond, Washington. When it began two years ago, the lead pastor, Darrell Waddell, was determined that the worship music would be of outstanding quality. In choosing to focus so intensely on music, Darrell knew that there would be some other things the church would not be able to do. Being in a new church allowed him the freedom to be specific. The result is that Cascade Hills has an incredible jazz worship team that attracts many people to their "worship café" service.

MULTIPLICATION

Rabbits are known for being prolific breeders. Leave a male and female rabbit together, and you'll soon have lots of little bunnies. Something similar happens with church plants—they tend to be prolific at reproducing themselves. When churches begin to parent reproducing churches, the number of churches in an area increases dramatically in a short time.

In 1997 there were ten Wesleyan churches in northern California with a combined worship attendance of about 1,500. Those ten churches received contributions totaling $1,389,968 and provided $124,632 in support to the denomination. In 1998, a church parenting movement began in that region, and existing churches began to parent reproducing churches. By 2003 the ten churches had multiplied to twenty and had a combined worship attendance of approximately 2,500. They received contributions totaling $2,867,029 and provided $197,072 in support of their denomination. When churches begin to reproduce, they usually continue.

Is it impossible for established churches to incorporate these effectiveness factors into their evangelism strategies? Of course not. But established churches will never be as effective at evangelism as new churches. Senior adults can get in good physical condition and even run marathons. But older people will never run as well as younger ones. Youth has energy. That's true for churches as well. All congregations, regardless of age, should be winning people to Christ. Yet we must recognize the evangelistic vitality of new congregations and do all we can to capitalize upon it. New churches reach more people for Christ. Therefore, planting churches is the single most effective method of evangelism.

WHAT TO DO ABOUT IT

Perhaps you have never entertained the idea of parenting a church. You may have determined that God called you to build a single large church, not to parent new ones. Yet you may sense a change in your spirit. Perhaps you recognize that increasing the size of one congregation and planting new churches are not mutually exclusive aims. You may realize that church planting is an effective evangelistic method and feel prompted to participate.

This is the beginning of a God-given dream.

One day, Jesus planted a dream in the heart of Peter (see Luke 5:1–11). Jesus was teaching by the Sea of Galilee, and the crowds had pushed him to the water's edge. Jesus asked if he might sit in Peter's boat to teach, and Peter honored the request. But it was after Jesus had finished teaching that Peter's real lesson began.

Jesus asked Peter to push out into deep water and let his nets down for a catch. Peter was not thrilled by this suggestion. He had been fishing all night and was probably tired. He and his partners had been washing their nets when Jesus asked to use the boat. Tending the nets was their last activity for the day. In essence, Jesus was asking Peter to do something unexpected, something extra, and something that held little promise of success. He asked Peter to believe that there were fish to catch during the day when he had just fished all night—with no results.

Yet Peter accepted Jesus' invitation, and the resulting catch was so great that it nearly swamped the boat.

The dream of parenting churches is the dream of doing something unexpected, something that requires extra effort, something that—some would say—holds little promise of success. It is a dream that involves investing people, finances, and resources. It is a dream that involves influencing an entire region through multiplication. Jesus invites us to dream of letting our nets down in deep water. If he has planted that dream in your heart, hold on to it. Cultivate it. Write down the inner nudges that you feel. Ask God to clarify these promptings. Drive through your area envisioning the possibilities. Talk to church leaders who have parented or planted churches.

Then go—into the deep water—and let down your net for a catch.

CHAPTER FOUR

MODELS

OF PARENTING

———〰〰———

RIPPLE PRINCIPLE
There are many ways to parent churches.

T here are two general types of church parenting: intentional and unintentional. There are examples of both types in Scripture, and either can result in a growing, healthy, and reproducing church.

The early church began in the city of Jerusalem, and the first believers might have stayed there if not for an unforeseen event—the persecution of the church. With the stoning of Stephen (see Acts 7), persecution broke out against the Christians in Jerusalem. As a result, they scattered. Believers moved across the Mediterranean region practicing this basic evangelistic principle: Where we are is where we share. As they scattered, these Christians actually gathered a harvest of new believers who needed new churches to nurture them and help them mature. These churches were started *unintentionally.*

Some scattered believers found themselves in Antioch (Acts 11:19–21). The local church in that city became an epicenter of multiplication. Barnabas brought Paul there to help the local ministry.

53

Later, the leadership of the Antioch church recognized the spiritual need of unreached people in the cities surrounding them, so they commissioned Paul and Barnabas to go on an evangelistic journey (Acts 13:1–3). Through this sending act, the Antioch church *intentionally* started a church parenting movement.

In the twenty-first century, both unintended circumstances and intentional actions are still being used by God to create new congregations. Which model would work best in your situation? You decide.

INTENTIONAL PARENTING MODELS

Intentional parenting occurs when believers, prompted by the Holy Spirit, create a plan to initiate a new congregation. This merger of spiritual guidance and strategic planning probably creates the best circumstances for the birthing of a healthy reproducing congregation. Here are nine suggested models for intentional church parenting.

DAUGHTERING

When most people hear the word *Kleenex,* they think of a disposable facial tissue. To them, that's what the word means. In fact, *Kleenex* is the trade name for one brand of facial tissues. *Xerox* is a similar term. To many, the word *Xerox* means photocopy. But the word is really a trademark for one company that makes photocopy equipment. In the field of church parenting, the term *daughtering* has gained similar dominance. For most people, that term is synonymous with the idea of church parenting.

Daughtering is when a single local church initiates and leads the creation of a new congregation. In this model, the parent church assumes the primary responsibility for finding a church planter, funding the project, and guiding the early stages of the new church's ministry. In the initial phases, the daughter church is often seen as an extension of the parent church's ministry. When this model is used, the parent church may receive assistance from a denomination or association, but the local church has the responsibility for initiating and fulfilling the plans. Ideally, each daughter church would be encouraged to become a parent church once it was strong and healthy.

In September 2003, Kingswood Church in Blaine, Minnesota, parented North Point Church. Kingswood, under the leadership of Pastor Al Goracke, brought on a planting pastor, and the parent church provided housing, training, and coaching for him. The planter was given permission to recruit Kingswood members to join the core team for the daughter church. Kingswood's denomination provided financial resources and much-needed encouragement, and the project succeeded beautifully. "Revitalization came to Kingswood Church because of the decision to plant other churches," Pastor Goracke reports. "This renewed energy given to fulfilling the Great Commission enabled Kingswood to experience a new vitality that could only come from God."[1]

Just as Kleenex is only one type of facial tissue, daughtering is only one method of parenting a church. A true movement cannot be limited in its creativity.

SHARED PARENTING

Shared parenting is when two or more congregations work together to parent a church. The congregations combine their resources, but typically, one of them takes the lead. This model is an outstanding option for smaller churches with limited resources or in an area in which several churches surround a strategic community.

West Sacramento, California, sits across the river from downtown. Several churches in the Sacramento Area have a burden for West Sacramento. They are combining their efforts with their denomination to plant a church in that vicinity. These congregations share the load financially, organizationally, and relationally. Their shared parenting will result in an effective new church.

SATELLITES

A *satellite* is an off-campus ministry begun by a local church with the eventual goal of producing an organized, self-sustaining congregation.

The satellite campus remains part of the parent church's organization until it is financially and organically strong enough to stand on its own. This model of parenting has a low impact on the mother church.

In Vista, a small community in Southern California, Vista Wesleyan Church, averaging fewer than one hundred saw several of its families move to a fast-growing area thirty-five miles northeast. Rather than viewing the circumstances as a loss, the church's leaders chose to view the circumstances through the lens of church multiplication. They began a satellite campus, using the families that had moved away as the core group. The parent church supplied a worship team, children's ministry workers, and other leaders. The parent church pastor preached at both campuses until the satellite became strong enough to support its own pastor. Eventually, the satellite church brought on its own pastor, and the small core group expanded to a congregation of more than forty people.

MULTICAMPUSES

The *multicampus* model is similar to the satellite model with one major difference: in the multicampus approach, there is no intention to form a new self-supporting church. The additional campus (or campuses) has its own leadership, pastor, and ministry emphasis, but it remains part of the parent church's structure. Typically, the campus pastors are staff members of the parent church.

Horizon Christian Fellowship is a large church in San Diego County. In 1985 it leased a junior high school and developed a growing ministry there. In 1993, seeing a need to reach beyond one campus—literally—the church leased an elementary school that was approximately two miles away. The second campus is staffed by its own ministry team and functions separately from the main campus. In the beginning senior pastor Mike McIntosh preached at both locations; however, he eventually turned the preaching responsibilities at the elementary school campus over to a staff pastor. Horizon's willingness to approach ministry with a parenting mind-set enables them to reach even more people.

A strong rural church might consider reaching surrounding communities via this model. Such congregations often already attract people from several small towns. A church might more effectively reach those communities by beginning campuses in them.

COLONIZATION

This model is seldom used, but it is appropriate for some churches. *Colonization* entails the relocation of a core team to a distant community by a parent church. This is a costly and challenging model because core team members must move, get jobs, and establish new homes and relationships in the planting area.

Kentwood Community Church in Grand Rapids, Michigan, had a staff member with a burden for the Metro-Atlanta Area. This parent church helped to relocate him and a few other pioneering families to Atlanta, where they started a church. Fifteen years later, Crossroad Community Church in Lawrenceville, Georgia, is averaging close to three thousand in weekend attendance, thanks to the courage and sacrifice of the Michigan congregation.

RESTARTING

A local church, in partnership with denominational leadership, comes alongside a struggling congregation. The struggling congregation is first closed and then *restarted*. The goal is to recreate a healthy, growing, reproducing church with a new mission and vision.

In Yuba City, California, several families left a small congregation. At about the same time, the long-tenured pastor retired. These circumstances combined to put the church in a downward spiral. The members decided to close the church.

Shortly afterward, denominational leaders found that a small band of people wanted to restart the church. They were organized into a core group, and a pastor was assigned to help them in this endeavor. Services were begun, a new name was selected, and the congregation developed a new mission statement and core values. Today, it is a growing church.

LANGUAGE GROUP CONGREGATIONS

An existing church may parent a congregation by targeting a specific *language group*. Immigrants arrive in North America every day, many of whom have a desire to maintain their ethnic identity. Starting congregations for non-English speakers is a way to do cross-cultural ministry without ever leaving the country!

Neighborhood Christian Fellowship in West Covina, California, saw that the community around them was changing. Several ethnic groups were making this area their home. The leadership of Neighborhood Christian Fellowship determined to reach the newcomers, and identified target groups. The parent church brought in ethnic pastors to minister to the unique needs of the immigrant population, and began churches on their property.

INSIDE-OUT PLANTING

Greenwood Community Church in Indianapolis began an alternative service in its old sanctuary, which was also located on its main campus. This service had a style all its own. The only resemblance it shared with the main service was that Dr. Charles Lake, the senior pastor spoke at both. After several months, Dr. Lake realized that he didn't enjoy the style of the alternate service. He suggested that the youth pastor take leadership of the service with the eventual goal of starting a new church. This new church continues to meet in the old sanctuary, has its own budget, board of elders, and strategic approach to ministry. In fact, this new congregation now has plans to parent a church in the inner city of Indianapolis.

HOUSE CHURCHES

A *house church*, as the name implies, is a church that meets in a private home. House churches provide an excellent way to involve bivocational ministers or lay leaders in church planting. The cost is minimal, and the potential for rapid multiplication is incredible.

House churches are not glorified Bible studies. They have the elements of a fully functioning body of believers. A house church is a group of believers committed to the Bible, fellowship, breaking of bread, and prayer, as identified in Acts 2:42.[2] The challenge for parenting churches and denominational entities is to allow a definition of *church* that will accommodate this new generation of children. Most house congregations will never become large or own property, but they can still function as viable local expressions of Christian fellowship, worship, and outreach. They hold the advantage of being highly relational and having a high degree of accountability.

In Mill Bay, British Columbia, a planter is beginning a parenting movement one house at a time. His vision is to establish a network of house churches led by bivocational pastors. These churches will meet independently but gather for community celebrations.

THE NEXT PARADIGM

The next paradigm doesn't exist yet. It is an innovative model for church parenting that God is germinating in the heart of a church leader—maybe you. As church leaders gain a parenting mentality, more and more models for multiplying congregations will be developed. Only God knows where these innovations will take the church.

UNINTENTIONAL PARENTING MODELS

Unintentional church parenting happens when a local church embraces and supports a new congregation that it did not choose to initiate. Sometimes that requires applying God's grace to a potentially destructive situation. Unintentional church parenting may result from five types of situations.

SPLAT

When an impending church split results in the creation of a viable congregation, the result might be termed a *splat* (split into a plant). A splat will leave some people hurt and a bit disconnected, but a healthy, reproducing church can be born out of adverse conditions. My friend Mark Williams says that in such a scenario, a church may resemble an alley cat. It shrieks and screams all night long, but in the morning, the result is more cats!

In the expansive Greater Bay Area of northern California, an established church began to experience conflict between the pastor and some longstanding leaders. It became evident that either the pastor would have to go, which would result in a number of people leaving the church, or the pastor would stay, which would drive some leading families away from the church. Efforts were made to reconcile the parties, but it seemed the congregation was on a fast track to a split.

Finally, denominational leaders suggested that the pastor leave and begin another church five miles away. Any person who wanted to join him could go along. In the end, what had threatened to be an acrimonious split became an amicable parting. A new church was birthed.

ADOPTION

Occasionally, an independent group of worshipers looks for a place where they can find support and encouragement. Another local church may embrace such a group and help them establish leadership and organizational support. The daughter group already exists and is *adopted* by the parent church.

A group of second-generation Asian Americans was meeting in a Bible study and had a vision to reach their network of acquaintances for Christ. They had come from a denomination that did not support them in fulfilling that vision. Leaders of the group approached a local church of another denomination and requested assistance. This local church adopted the small group of neighbors. The adoptive parent church helped them find a pastor and gave them financial support and guidance to get established. Today, this small Bible study has become a growing congregation that is committed to reproducing.

Questions that a parent church should consider with a prospective adoptee are listed in Appendix A.

DEATH AND REBIRTH

There are times, fortunately rare, when a mother dies in childbirth. That mother literally gives her life for her child. That can happen in church parenting too, when one church dies to give life to another. An existing church may have dwindled to a point of ineffectiveness. The people of this church courageously decide to close their doors. They sell the church property and use the assets to begin a new church. One church dies so another might live.

In Madison, Wisconsin, Good Shepherd, an older, dwindling church made this choice. It was in an older part of town and had fewer than thirty active members. In cooperation with denominational leaders, the church sold its property and the assets were used to fund a new, cutting-edge church in a growing part of the city. Because of the sacrificial death of Good Shepherd, Lakeshore Community was born.

SURPRISE

My friends Tim and Sandy thought they were done having children. Their youngest was entering junior high, and they looked forward to the freedom that they would soon enjoy. Everything was fine until they discovered that Sandy was pregnant. Surprise!

The birth of another child was not part of their plan, but Tim and Sandy were ideally suited to the challenge. They had a support structure in place. They had a home. They had maturity. They even had in-home babysitters! Tim did a great job holding up under the Father

Abraham wisecracks we made. Although news of the pregnancy came as a shock to them, neither Tim nor Sandy would ever think of giving Kevin back. He is a great addition to their family. Just because a pregnancy comes as a surprise doesn't mean it won't be welcome. The same is true when church parenting comes as a surprise.

In 2001 I took over pastoral leadership of Spring Valley Church in Rocklin, California, a church that was just four years old. Mark Welch, the planting pastor had asked me to join the church as the lead pastor and volunteered to become my assistant. When I arrived, we talked about the possibility of him and his wife starting another church. Spring Valley Church, under the leadership of Pastor Mark Welch, had already parented two churches in its first four years of existence, and we felt it could parent again in two or three years.

After I had been at Spring Valley for a little over seven months, Pastor Mark approached me. He was ready to plant again. The timing was a surprise for me. I had not anticipated it so soon. But the congregation was committed to reproducing itself, so we pulled alongside and gave all the help we could. In January 2003, BridgePointe Church was launched in El Dorado Hills, a community fifteen miles southeast of the parent church. Spring Valley increased its ministry influence by responding positively to this surprise birth.

SURROGATE PARENTING

Surrogate parenting is a model for church planting that is initially spearheaded by a denomination, association, or some other organization other than a local church. A local church is then recruited to provide support for the new congregation. Four keys to successful surrogate parenting of a church are to establish clear roles for the district, the planter, and the surrogate parent; to develop timeframes for recruiting core members and a target date for the new church to launch; to negotiate accountability structures, clarifying who answers to whom; and to communicate the benefits of being a surrogate parent.

In Ohio a district supervisor approached Cypress Wesleyan Church with the idea of parenting a congregation. The supervisor had a planter and funds to start the church. All that was needed was a womb to nurture the envisioned church. The parent church would allow the planter to recruit core team members. The parent church planter would mentor the planter. The surrogate agreed, and today CrossLink Community Church is a growing congregation.

ART MORE THAN SCIENCE

Intentionally or unintentionally, churches need to parent new churches. *How* it is done is not nearly as important as *that* it is done. I've heard it said that life isn't a science; we make it up as we go along. The same can be said for parenting churches. It is more of an art than a science.

When creating a work of art, the artist needs a medium (paint, lead, ink), a surface (canvas, paper, wall), and an applicator (brush, pen, airbrush). The artist brings these elements together in a unique way. No two works of art are exactly the same.

Those who read these pages will have come from different locations, situations, and backgrounds. In that mix of people, circumstances, and challenges, there is an opportunity to create something unique—a new congregation. Each of us has the opportunity to use what we have to meet the great need in the lives of people. Our canvases differ, but each is ready to be covered with God-given creativity and innovation.

There is no single right response to the challenge of parenting a new congregation. Let the Holy Spirit guide you in creating a work of art that brings glory to his name.

CHAPTER FIVE

BARRIERS TO
CHURCH PARENTING

—⚊⚊—

It wasn't big. It wasn't fancy. It wasn't in a great location. It wasn't all that expensive. It wasn't a lot of things. But the one thing it was made up for all it wasn't—it was ours! Joni and I had rented a number of apartments and various houses, and they were fine. They were adequate shelter, but we never got terribly excited about them. On the day we moved into our own home, our attitude changed. We took pride in our home. We took special care of it. We had long-term plans for this house, and it showed. That shift in attitude is typical when people go from renting a home to owning one.

Something similar happens when people take ownership of nearly anything—including a vision for church parenting. Until pastors, board members, and other influence makers in the local church own a vision for parenting, they will lack enthusiasm.

Rented vision is enthusiasm based on the desire or energy of another. When other leaders appear to be excited about church parenting, a not-so-enthused leader may feel some responsibility to support the effort. That support is usually nominal and short-lived because those who rent the vision will always see church parenting as a mandate from outside the local church rather than as their own responsibility. Rented vision usually results in empty words of affirmation and token financial support. They also agree that there is a need for more churches, but they do not take responsibility for creating them. Need alone does not create a burden. There are needs everywhere, and local leaders realize that they cannot meet every need effectively.

Multiplication happens when local congregations buy into the vision for church parenting. Ownership changes attitudes, availability, action—everything. So how is ownership of a vision created? What is the process by which local leaders purchase the vision for themselves? It begins with the pastor. Without realizing it, he or she may be the first obstacle to church multiplication.

RELUCTANT LEADERSHIP

In the days when logs were floated downriver to a sawmill, they sometimes got tangled and clogged, causing a logjam. In many cases, a logjam could be cleared by removing just one log. That log was the key to restoring movement. A novice logger would have searched for the source of the jam by going out on the river and jiggling logs until he found the key log. The approach was time consuming and dangerous. A more experienced logger, however, would have moved away from the river's edge to a high spot of ground, a place from which he could survey the entire logjam. From that vantage point, the logger could see the key log, then go and move it. When the key log moved, the entire flow followed.

When there is a barrier in casting the vision for church planting or parenting, the senior pastor is usually the key to resolving it. When he or she catches the vision, others follow. If the pastor is hesitant, the congregation will be too. Many pastors lack the vision for church multiplication because they simply have never given it serious consideration. If that describes you, take the time to explore this movement. Give this mandate due consideration before making up your mind about it. The first step in doing that is to seek God through prayer.

PRAY ABOUT CHURCH MULTIPLICATION

One of the clearest examples of leadership in the Bible is Nehemiah, who was used by God to lead the people of Israel in an aggressive renovation project. Nehemiah was the catalyst behind their vision to rebuild the walls of Jerusalem. The Old Testament book of Nehemiah provides a clinic in the art of planning, leading, and managing change in the midst of adversity.

In the first four verses of Nehemiah, we discover the secret of his leadership: *he got on his knees.* Prayer is the secret to success in any Kingdom endeavor. The first step in exploring the possibility of church parenting is to get before God and ask "What, if anything, do you want me to do in this area?"

The problem confronting Jerusalem was one of security. The city's walls had been broken down and its gates burned with fire (Neh. 1:3). This was no condition for a city, but was it Nehemiah's problem? Remember that need alone does not constitute a burden. Jerusalem's need for security did not automatically become Nehemiah's responsibility. He didn't even live there. In fact, he had never been to Jerusalem. He had a good position serving the king of a distant land. Things were running smoothly. Finances were adequate. Why would Nehemiah spend time and energy on a community in which he had little personal investment? Besides, Nehemiah was a cupbearer by training, something like a foodservice manager. He wasn't a builder.

As pastors, we often find ourselves in a similar situation to Nehemiah's. We are fulfilled in our ministries; things are going well. We're good at what we do and are busy with the affairs of a local church. The people in our congregations are being challenged and changed. So why bother doing something (church parenting) that we've never been trained to do in a place we've never been? While acknowledging the need for more churches, a pastor may well ask, "What does that have to do with me?"

Nehemiah's response was to pray about the situation. He wrote, "When I heard these things [the condition of Jerusalem], I sat down and wept. For some days I mourned and fasted and prayed before the God of heaven" (Neh.1:4). It's interesting that Nehemiah didn't immediately jump on the go-rebuild-Jerusalem bandwagon. Nor did he simply dismiss the situation as none of his concern. He fasted and prayed. His decision—whatever it would be—would be made on his knees. His reaction to the need would not be based on his personal goals, his "ministry wedge," or his preferred geographic location. It would be based on prayer. Everything that follows in the book of Nehemiah is birthed in verse four, Nehemiah's prayer.

It is true that need alone does not constitute a burden, yet many pastors never even enter a discussion about church parenting. They either dive into the church multiplication wave or jump out of its way. Maybe it's time to discuss the matter with the one whose opinion matters most—God. As leaders, we need to enter his presence and honestly seek his direction. As Floyd Tidsworth puts it, "Prayer should saturate the whole effort of starting a church."[1]

If you've never seriously considered the idea of church parenting, I urge you to do so. Get out your PDA, date book, or whatever you use to track appointments, and locate a day in the next two weeks when you have a minimum of four hours available. Block out that time to spend seeking the will of God. Go to a place where you will have no interruptions. Take a Bible and something to write with, but leave your cell phone or pager at home. Spend the time reading the book of Acts and asking God for wisdom. Focus on this question: "Lord, what, if anything, do you want me to do in the area of church multiplication?"

SET ASIDE DEFINITIONS OF "SUCCESS"

In order to give church multiplication fair consideration, pastors must learn to think beyond the traditional measures of success used in the church. Success tends to be measured by three B's: *buildings, bodies,* and *budgets.* In each of these areas, the goal is to have more. The perceived value of these measures is underscored by the applause and attention given to pastors of larger churches. Most pastors, regardless of what size church they pastor, eventually come to feel that they must produce an ever-larger congregation in order to be successful in the ministry.

There is nothing inherently wrong about wanting to build a great church for God, even if that greatness is measured by the three B's. But the kingdom of God cannot be bounded by a church's property line. Pastors whose desire for church growth becomes a fixation on their own ministry will inevitably concentrate their work on one church in one place instead of parenting multiple churches in multiple locations.

Dr. Mark Williams of Dynamic Church Planting International[2] once told me, "Churches that plant churches need a pastor with a real vision for the lost and a complete lack of selfishness." It takes an unselfish leader to look beyond one's own church. It takes an unselfish leader to invest people and resources into a ministry from which his or her own congregation may not benefit directly. Pastor, open your mind to the possibility that your greatest success may be your investment in the ministry of others. Allow yourself to break free from the confining notion that your building, attendance average, and budget are the only measures of your effectiveness. Take time to get on your knees and seek God. Open yourself to his leading and prompting. You are the key to creating a vision for church multiplication within your congregation.

THE COST OF INVESTING

I am not a financial wizard. I don't track the stock market. My few investments are in mutual funds, which I pretty much leave alone. But even I know that it is better for investments to increase in value rather than to decrease. No one would intentionally place money in a portfolio knowing it would result in a loss. That's why many pastors are slow to adopt the idea of church parenting—they see it as a loss for their congregations.

Church parenting *is* costly, but that cost is an investment, not a loss. There is a cost to investing in the stock market, but those who buy stocks are not throwing money away. Their goal is to get a return. They hope to make money, not lose it. In the same way, church parenting is an investment in the Kingdom. Churches that parent other churches do not lose. They do not lose money; they invest it into a situation that will result in a net return to the Kingdom. They do not lose people; they invest them in the work of gathering a harvest. Is that mere semantics? No. It is a difference in mind-set, a difference in attitude. If a local church views church planting as a loss to itself, it will never embrace a parenting project. To successfully multiply, a congregation must view church parenting as an investment in the Kingdom.

When Arcade Wesleyan Church parented its first daughter church, Arcade invested fifty-five people. This was roughly 15 percent of its Sunday morning congregation. Occasionally, people who remained at Arcade would say, "We lost some of our key people!" But I would put up my hand to keep them from going on, then correct them by saying, "We didn't lose them; we invested them. The Kingdom will get a return." Soon we began to laugh about it. When chatting about the church plant, people would catch themselves starting to say "lost" and quickly change to "invest." I caught myself on several occasions.

What investment is required of a parent church? There are five resources that a congregation must be willing to part with in order to parent a church. I call them the *Five M's*.

MEMBERS

A parent church may invest members in a church plant. Many people who are active in congregational life will respond to the opportunity to help establish a new congregation. Often, these volunteers will be the cream of the crop. Why do the best and the brightest respond to challenges? They have a high degree of buy-in to the church's mission and they have a bring-it-on mentality.

Core members of a congregation are the first to buy into the vision because they want to expand their church's ministry influence. They recognize early that church parenting is central to the work of the Kingdom, and they want to support it. They see church parenting as part of the mission of the local church. These people typically have the attitude of Caleb, who said to Joshua, "Give me this hill country" (Josh. 14:12). They want to explore new ministry territory and are prepared to be uncomfortable for God.

Mark was a board member and a lead Sunday school teacher at Arcade Wesleyan Church. I had the privilege of discipling him, and he'd been in an accountability group with me for four years. He was a leader, a friend, and a confidant. Standing in the church parking lot one day, he told me that he and his wife Danielle were going to go help begin Spring Valley Church, Arcade's third parenting effort. I can still hear his exact words: "This is the right thing to do. Besides, I am ready for a *new challenge*."

Quality leaders are always ready to go and be used, and you must let them go. To be successful in church parenting, you must be willing to release key church members into the care of another. That is never easy, but it is right. Be unselfish. Hold your church's human resources loosely. Be willing to invest them in the Kingdom.

Sometimes I'm asked, "Have you had disgruntled people leave your church to join a church planting effort?" My honest response is, "No, unfortunately!" Church parenting does not clear the deadwood from a congregation. It harvests the best fruit. Disgruntled members will stay and continue to be your humbling agent. May God bless you both.

Of course, not all of the best people will leave to join a church parenting team. Some will stay. God lays on the hearts of many the call to remain at the parent church and strengthen it. In 2000 Jim

Bogear planted The River Church in Sacramento, California, as a daughter of Arcade Wesleyan Church. When he began to recruit the core team from Arcade, he helped the congregation understand the call of planting. He let it be known that the call was for everyone. God calls some to go and grow a new church. God calls others to stay and stabilize the parent. Regardless, they are called!

Keep looking for those who can be developed into leaders. Cultivate people intentionally and regularly. Create leadership incubators to nurture potential leaders. All leaders in the church should recruit and develop others so that there will be someone to fill their shoes if they are called to step out into a new venture.

MONEY

A parent church invests money in its daughter from two sources: the tithe of the core team members and parental gifts.

When people are invested in a new venture, their giving goes with them. The tithe of core team members provides the new church its initial financial footing. Never does a church live more on the ragged edge of faith than when it risks its finances. It is interesting that we tell others to trust God in their personal finances, but we quiver at the prospect of trusting God corporately. Do we really believe what we preach?

In one of the churches that I helped launch, two of the top five financial contributors to the parent church were called to go. One was the single largest giver, an entrepreneurial businessman. He not only gave regularly throughout the year but also provided a special year-end gift. He was a board member, a leader, and a person of influence. Honestly, investing his influence and leadership didn't concern me as much as giving up his financial contribution. When I discovered that his family was called to go with the daughter church, I asked God, "OK, how are you going to pull this off?"

Within one week I received a phone call from a young couple. A few months earlier, I'd had the privilege of helping Diane back to the

Lord and leading her husband Jeff into a relationship with Jesus. They had been attending our church for less than six months. They asked to see me that day, and an hour later they were seated in my office.

"I've been listening to your sermon tape on tithing," Jeff began, "and we want to do that. How do we start?"

I reminded them what tithing was, explained how to use the church's offering envelopes, and suggested that Sunday morning would be a good time to begin giving.

"We want to start that now," Jeff said, and he meant *now*. He opened his checkbook, wrote a check, placed it in one of the offering envelopes I'd given him, and handed it to me. I was startled by their passion but had enough presence of mind to pray with them before they left. Later, I glanced at the outside of the envelope. The amount was significant, and I thought they might have made a mistake. Although I wouldn't normally do this, I decided to open the envelope to be sure the amount was correct. It was. Obviously, this couple was making up for lost time and giving several weeks' worth of tithe at once.

While their contribution did not replace that of the two families who were joining the daughter church, God used the occasion to remind me that he would provide for all our needs. It might take several families to replace the two who were leaving, but then, God had provided them in the first place—they were not mine to hold. As ministry leaders, our job is to release resources; it is God's job to replenish them.

MUD

Saddleback Community Church is a great church. It has a tremendous ministry in Southern California. Saddleback is a large church and still growing. Yet not everyone in the Saddleback Valley attends this church, nor will they. That may be one reason that Saddleback Community Church, under Pastor Rick Warren's leadership, participates in church planting (a little-known fact).

A parent church invests turf and territory—mud—into a daughtering effort. It's tempting to become arrogant and territorial in the ministry. We are arrogant to believe that only we can reach the community around us. We are territorial when we think no other church should encroach on our "God-given" area. Never mind that we have had many years to reach those around us and not done it effectively. There is nothing wrong, of course, with believing that you have a wonderful church and that everyone should want to attend it. I have always felt the same way about my own local church.

But not everyone does attend my church, and they never will. Church parenting acknowledges the fact that no one church will reach an entire community. We need a variety of churches to reach a variety of people. Invest mud. Release territory. My friend Dr. Mark Williams emphasized the need for that when he told me, "A pastor has to gain a Kingdom mind-set, a belief that the Lord is pleased with the harvest, even if it isn't in his own fields."

The church I most recently led parented three new churches. One meets in the same commercial building development as the parent, at about the same time, only a football field's distance away. Yet they minister to people the parent church would never reach, and the parent church reaches those whom the daughter would never attract. It is about the Kingdom, not the real estate.

MINISTRY RESOURCES

A parent church invests ministry resources in its daughter—the gifts, skills, and talents of the people whom they invest. People cannot go and leave their abilities behind. The good news is that God will raise up others in the parent congregation to meet its ministry needs. It's likely that they will be unexpected people whom God is even now grooming to fill the gap. Their gifts and skills will be manifested as they sense the call to stay and strengthen the parent.

Frank was our slam-dunk best instrumentalist. He had been a professional musician, playing in clubs around the Sacramento area.

When Jesus saved him, Frank began using his musical gift in the worship band at Arcade Wesleyan Church. Then God called him and his family to join one of our daughter churches. Releasing him was quite an investment.

Meanwhile, Kristen and her family had been attending our church for about one year. After one service she approached our worship team leader. She said she played the guitar and sang. She was almost apologetic, but she wanted to know if she could contribute. We soon discovered that Kristen was an accomplished guitarist who also wrote music. She became an incredible addition to our worship ministry. One day the team leader asked her, "Why have you waited so long to volunteer?" Kristen's response was telling. She said, "Until I realized that several on the worship team were going to the plant, I didn't think you needed me." Here was a resource we might never have cultivated if we had not been parenting a church.

It's like having a bullpen, the stable of relief pitchers on a baseball team. God holds people in reserve until just the right time. When relief is needed, he will call them out. Release your ministry resources. God will draw upon his bullpen to meet your need. Your team is deeper than you might think.

MOMENTUM

It would be a mistake to sugarcoat the cost of investing in a new church. The parent church must sacrifice momentum in order to create a daughter congregation. The parent congregation will gear down. When members, money, mud, and ministry resources are invested, there will be a lag in momentum. That natural phenomenon results from two contrasting feelings among the parent congregation. The first is incredible joy; the second is sorrow.

The joy comes from realizing that *We did it! God used us to begin a new work. Many people will be reached because of our investment. Our influence is expanding into areas we never dreamed possible.* Just as a sports team savors winning a championship, a parent church should bask in the parenting of a healthy church. There should be time for celebrating victories. Yet there will be a lull in the momentum even as the sweet success is enjoyed.

The second reaction is sorrow. That comes from the realization that *We did it! We parented this church! We invested friends and family to make it happen. There are faces we will not see for some time. Our relationships will change. They will be a part of us, but they will be apart from us.* Just as a new mother feels postpartum sadness along with excitement about the birth, a mother church feels sorrow about the loss and change within the parent church along with joy about the daughter's birth. Every church must process that sadness, first by acknowledging it. Feelings of loss do not negate the joy of the parenting. Second, every congregation needs time to recover from the stress of parenting a church. It must rest and focus on growing stronger. The week after launching a daughter church is not the time to introduce a multiphase building program. But the mixed emotions will pass.

THE GOD GAP

Parenting a church will stretch a congregation unlike few other things because it forces a church into the *God Gap*—the place where our resources stop and God's must start. Parent churches dwell in the God Gap.

Peter became a walking—and drowning—illustration of the God Gap when he stepped out to meet Christ on the water. Peter began within the comfortable confines of the boat; but when he saw Jesus walking on the water, Peter wanted to join him. As soon as Peter swung his leg out of the boat, his resources were exhausted. He needed God's help if he was to succeed.

When you make the decision to parent a new congregation, you step over the side of the boat. It's a scary moment, fraught with the potential for failure. But, like Peter, you will have entered the God Gap, that place where you can experience the touch of Jesus as never before. Are you ready? Step into the Gap.

CHAPTER SIX

MYTHS, HINDRANCES, AND HURDLES IN CHURCH PARENTING

—ⱳ—

> ### RIPPLE PRINCIPLE
> Ripple leaders foresee and plan for the
> obstacles to church parenting.

The rock has been thrown. The ripple is expanding. All appears to be well until you realize that something is impeding the ripple's progress. You were so focused on the point of impact that you did not notice the logs, fallen trees, and bushes that might hinder the wave's advancement. This debris impedes the motion of the expanding ripples. Will it halt altogether?

It doesn't have to. When ripples in a pond encounter some disruption, they don't stop—they go around. The ripple created by church multiplication is likely to encounter some obstacles, but they need not stop its progress. As a leader, you can minimize the effect of these negative factors if you recognize them, understand them, and are prepared to deal with them. These are the myths, hindrances, and hurdles of church parenting. Remove them, and you will increase the likelihood that your ripple will expand to the other shore.

MYTHS TO EXPOSE

Myths are false notions that are commonly accepted as true. For example, many of us were taught that George Washington once threw a dollar across the Potomac River. Although that never happened, many people continue to believe that it is true. A number of myths surround the church multiplication movement. These are fundamental misunderstandings of what is involved in a successful church parenting effort. These false notions have dissuaded many from attempting church planting or parenting. Here are four of the most common church parenting myths.

THE MYTH OF ATTENDANCE

The myth of attendance is the misconception that a congregation must be a certain size to successfully parent a church. Most local church leaders who resist church parenting believe that their church is either too small, too large, or too mid-sized to parent another church. Whatever their size, most church leaders believe it is the wrong one.

Yet parenting has little to do with a church's attendance; it depends much more on the church's attitude. It's not the size of the congregation but the size of its heart that counts. You can probably name an undersized athlete who excelled in spite of her small stature. "She's got heart!" is what we often say about such overachievers. Any church—large or small—that has a heart for reaching the lost can find the means to become involved in church parenting.

Pastors sometimes claim—perhaps as a way of putting off the issue—that they will attempt church parenting when their own congregation reaches a certain size. That rarely happens, however, because church parenting is not in their hearts. These pastors are like church members who claim they will begin tithing when their income reaches a certain level. They seldom do, because the issue is not their cash flow but their attitude about stewardship. In the same way, churches that have no heart for multiplication when they are small seldom acquire one as they grow larger.

But is there an optimum size for church parenting? Some church planting consultants believe that congregations averaging from one hundred to five hundred in attendance are the best size to parent a church. My own experience confirms that. Churches in that size range generally have the resources to parent and are not encumbered with debt. That puts them in an ideal position to invest people yet retain a critical mass.

That ideal range should not be taken as a firm boundary, however. Is there an ideal size for a wide receiver in the National Football League? Yes, but there are many accomplished receivers who don't fit the ideal profile. Churches of all sizes can participate in parenting.

THE MYTH OF AGE

Some leaders wrongly believe that only churches of a certain age can successfully parent a congregation. They have in mind the age of the institution, not the age of its members. Usually, such leaders believe that their church is too old to undertake a parenting project. Like a woman who believes that her "biological clock" has stopped ticking, some pastors think that even if they wanted to produce a daughter congregation, it's too late—their church is too old now.

It is true that a church is most apt to parent in its first three years of existence. That's because newer churches tend to be more adaptable. They have fewer traditions to contend with and no sacred cows to overcome. That is one reason, by the way, why it is so important to implant the idea of multiplication into the thinking—the DNA— of a daughter church. When a church is planted with the expectation that it will become a parent, and it is held accountable to that expectation, the results are powerful.

Yet the fact that young churches reproduce more readily does not mean that older congregations cannot or should not become involved in church multiplication. Older congregations often have more resources than younger ones. Youth has exuberance, but maturity has stability. Older congregations lend credibility to a movement. Regardless of their age, churches can multiply.

THE MYTH OF ACQUISITION

The myth of acquisition holds that a church must finish the big project on its horizon before it will be in a position to parent a congregation. That notion is revealed in statements like these:

- We will start a new congregation after our building project is completed.

- Once we've added a couple of staff members, we'll be in a position to try this.

- If we can increase our budget to X dollars, we'll try a church plant.

These churches always seem to have "one more thing" on their to-do list. Somehow they never quite get around to parenting a new congregation.

Yet it is possible for a congregation to do two things at once. It requires careful planning, but local expansion and church parenting can go hand in hand. The Arcade Wesleyan Church undertook a major renovation project during the same period of time that it parented three congregations. Adventure Christian Church is a megachurch in Roseville, California. The congregation is growing at an incredible rate and just completed a three-thousand-seat sanctuary. At the same time, this congregation has planted three churches and has plans for a fourth. Adventure Christian is a marvelous example of how local expansion and church multiplication can work together to impact a region.

Red Cedar Community Church is located in Rice Lake, Wisconsin. In the last two years, it has grown in an average weekend attendance from just over two hundred to nearly six hundred. At the same time, it has planted a daughter church in Cumberland, a small town fifteen miles away. Pastor Damian Williams told me, "The mindset among too many church leaders is that you have to decide between church growth and church multiplication. We are discovering that God's design is that they are both happening at the same time!"

It isn't either/or. Churches do not have to choose between growing local ministries and planting new churches. They can do both. After developing a willingness to invest outside themselves, most churches discover that they regain what they let go. They gain new converts, members, finances, and energy. Local growth is not the motivation for church parenting, but it can be a wonderful side effect.

THE MYTH OF ADEQUACY

I was sitting across the table from the pastor of a growing church in a metropolitan area. Over the years, he had led his congregation as it grew from a handful of people to more than two thousand. Now, he had a vision to parent three churches over the next five years. Although he was a proven leader with an excellent record, he confessed, "I have no idea how to go about this." Fortunately, that wouldn't hinder him from moving forward.

The myth of adequacy holds that church leaders must be experts in the art of church multiplication in order to become involved in church parenting. Some leaders use their lack of know-how as an excuse for not parenting. It is a poor one, though, given the ready availability of church planting consultants and tools. Resources are available. Churches at all levels of understanding can participate in a parenting effort. Lack of expertise should not be a barrier to involvement.

Which of these myths have prevented you from considering church parenting? Which do you hear most commonly among members of your congregation? How might you respond to them, now that you recognize them as false? Nearly every church can become involved in the church multiplication movement. No church should be left behind.

HINDRANCES TO AVOID

I pulled out of the driveway one day and began driving toward my office. As I drove along, the car seemed to labor more than usual. I sensed some resistance, almost as if something was holding me back. I continued along my way, but I knew that something wasn't right. After driving a couple of miles, I discovered that I had forgotten to release the parking brake. It's amazing how much easier a car moves when the brakes are off!

There are several hindrances that may put the brakes on a church planting movement. Like an engaged parking brake, they will not keep the movement from progressing, but they will cause it to labor unnecessarily. When you understand these hindrances, it is much easier to cast them off and continue moving freely. Here are seven hindrances to church parenting—and how to avoid them.

FOCUSING ON HEALTH FOR HEALTH'S SAKE

In recent years there has been a shift in emphasis from church growth to church health. Much of the credit for that is due to the incredible work of Christian Schwarz in his book *Natural Church Development*. Health is a crucial characteristic for a successful parent church, and healthy churches are more likely to participate in church multiplication. Yet health may become a hindrance to church parenting when a church focuses on health for health's sake. Some congregations become virtual hypochondriacs, monitoring their health so closely that they are unwilling to do anything else. Truly healthy churches are not self-focused. A byproduct of their healthy condition is a willingness to invest energy in others.

A WELFARE MENTALITY

Some church leaders resist planting new churches because they want to help existing churches that are not doing well. "Why use our money to start new churches?" they wonder. "Don't we have an obligation to help the churches we already have?"

The root of this thinking is the notion that money will solve any problem. Denominations and associations that continue to pour money into struggling or dying churches unwittingly create a welfare mentality. The result is that problems are perpetuated rather than alleviated. Struggling churches seldom lack money alone. While it is true that the need to plant new churches does not preempt the need to help existing ones, it is equally true that the need of a struggling congregation does not nullify the mandate to create new, healthy churches. To liberally paraphrase Jesus, "Struggling churches you will always have with you."

TERRITORIALISM

Planting new churches is sometimes perceived as an infringement on the territory of others who are trying to reach a given community. Squatters may not be welcomed.

Yet there are more people in any community than any one church can reach. Usually, existing churches in a given location have had decades—even centuries—to evangelize their communities. New churches will reach people that these existing congregations never have and perhaps never will. It is a mistake to put the needs of lost people on hold until existing churches find the right time and the right program to reach them.

THE "FILL 'ER UP" MIND-SET

I lived through the gas crisis of the 1970s—as did millions of others. During that time, many gas stations were open only on certain days. In some places, cars with even-numbered license plates could buy gas on some days and those with odd-numbered plates on other days. Long lines at filling stations were common, and many drivers became worried when their gas gauges dipped below half. When it was my day to fill up, I did not like to see other cars at the filling station. After all, they were after the same limited resource that I needed.

Some leaders bring a similar mind-set to the discussion of church multiplication. They want to see existing churches filled before adding new ones. "When the churches we have are bursting at the seams," they reason, "we'll consider planting new ones."

That never happens, of course. We will never fill up all of the existing churches in any denomination or in any community. The best way to increase our capacity is to add more containers, not to fill existing ones to the brim. We must not allow an unreachable goal (filling all existing churches to capacity) to hinder us from pursuing an achievable one (planting new churches).

DOING WHAT GETS REWARDED

While I served on John Maxwell's staff at Skyline Wesleyan Church, he told staff members, "What gets rewarded is what gets done." This is true in all organizations, including denominations. What gets rewarded in most denominations is an increase in the three B's: buildings, bodies, and budgets. Churches that are increasing in attendance, adding staff or facilities, or gaining income are singled out for applause. In spite of a growing emphasis on church health, growth is still the goal among leaders of most denominations. We reward pastors who are able to gather more people at one place at one time.

The urge to do what gets rewarded is a hindrance to church multiplication because church parenting is not on the applause list for most denominations. Often, denominations place unintentional barriers in the path of parent churches. For instance, churches that undertake a local building project may be allowed to pay a reduced amount in denominational support for a period of time. Such incentives are seldom offered to churches that undertake a parenting project. The not-so-subtle message is that denominations value real estate construction but not church multiplication.

Leaders who become involved in church multiplication must shake off the temptation to do only what gets rewarded. Their ultimate motivation is found in the Lord's words, "Well done, good and faithful servant." However, a human pat on the back doesn't hurt as we move toward the heavenly standing ovation. When denominations or organizations begin to applaud—and financially back—congregations that choose to multiply, more churches will get involved in church parenting.

FEAR OF RESPONSIBILITY

Maternity wards are full of life, but they are also full of challenges. Babies are messy. As they grow, children both delight and disturb their parents. Infants bring both lots of joy and lots of hard work. New churches are much the same. Many congregations resist parenting because they don't want to deal with the mess, the work, or the frustration of brining new life into the world. Leaders must overcome the fear of responsibility—both in themselves and in their congregations—in order to successfully parent a new church.

AVOIDING RISK

Church planting will never have a 100 percent success rate. Some new congregations won't make it. Church leaders generally realize that and often fear the possibility of failure. Why put so much effort into something that may not work? Yet all worthwhile endeavors carry some risk. Church planting is both worthwhile and risky. Where there is fear, the best response is faith. Leaders must be willing to risk their resources—and their reputations—and trust God for the result.

Hindrances should not be dismissed; they must be addressed. Like parking brakes, these hindrances have a legitimate function—they raise appropriate cautions. When I discovered that my parking brake was still engaged, I didn't disassemble it. I merely disengaged it because it was not useful at that point in my journey. Understand and recognize the attitudes described here. Allow them to be appropriate cautions, but never let them become hindrances to the work that God wants to do in your region through you.

HURDLES TO CLEAR

I was on the track and field team in high school, where I competed in the heavy events of shot put and discus. A friend of mine competed in the low and high hurdles. One day at practice, I asked him for a quick lesson. He gave me a few tips, and I gave it a try. The result wasn't good, however. In fact, I am lucky to be here to write about it! My inexperience in knowing how to navigate the hurdles resulted in pain both physical (from hitting them) and emotional (from the laughter of friends). That experience convinced me that I would make an excellent shot-putter.

An experienced hurdler can clear those obstacles gracefully, almost effortlessly. When you understand the technique and have some experience, hurdles aren't so difficult to cross. That's true in church parenting as well. There are hurdles—obstacles to success. If you hit them unprepared, pain is the likely result. With a little training, though, you can clear them gracefully.

FEAR

Church parenting may cause two types of fear. The first is internal. It manifests itself in questions about the parent church's ability to invest in the project and recover from it. Will the parent continue to grow? Will it be healthy? The second fear is external and raises questions about the daughter congregation. Will the new church make it? Will it grow and be healthy? I vividly remember lying awake the night before my oldest child's first day of school. I couldn't sleep as I worried whether I had done all I could to prepare him for the rigors of kindergarten. It was heart-rending. A parent church may experience that same anxiety for her child.

Those fears are natural, but they should not form a barrier to church parenting. They may be overcome by courage and faith. I like the statement "When fear knocks at the door, let faith answer." The fear of parenting is real, but we can step over it.

FINANCES

Financing church plants will be dealt with in detail in a later chapter, but I mention it here because it is a hurdle that must be crossed. Leaders must identify and cultivate income streams that will support the parenting effort. The problem really concerns creativity more than finances. Churches find the money to do what they value. Financing is an issue that must be addressed, but it should not become a barrier to participation in church multiplication.

PERSONALITY SHIFT

A church's personality results from the collective spirit of those whom God has placed within its walls. So when a congregation invests people in a church plant, the parent church's personality shifts. This can disrupt the congregation, but does not necessarily bring a negative result.

The minister of music in the church I most recently pastored felt called to plant a church. When he left, the worship team remained intact. We had the same keyboard player, drummer, lead guitarist, and vocalists. The quality of the music remained strong, but the feel was different. The church had to adjust to this shift in personality.

Changes in the parent church's personality can be challenging, but they are certainly not life threatening. Treat them as hurdles to be overcome with energy and spirit.

DENOMINATIONAL PERCEPTION

In my denomination, pastors and lay leaders gather for an annual district conference where we celebrate the previous year's achievements.

One of the report systems we use is a graph that shows the growth pattern for each church in our district. When a church invests people and resources into a daughter church, there is an excellent chance that the graph will show a downturn. To those who don't know—or don't care—that the church has invested itself in multiplication, it will appear that the church is unhealthy. Why else would people leave?

Overcoming the hurdle of misperception requires inner strength. Church leaders must be more convinced that their investment in parenting is worthwhile than they are concerned about their reputation among their peers. A ripple church must be self-confident. It must accept the fact that other leaders may not value what it is doing.

TIMING

Timing is everything. The timing of a comment from one spouse to another can make the difference between a good discussion and a heated argument. Timing can also make the difference between an effective church plant and a failed effort.

The first daughter church that I was involved in creating was launched four months before the original target date. The parent was more prepared for this birth than either the planter or I had anticipated. We realized that waiting for an artificial launch date would hinder our momentum, so we elected to launch early. The church had a successful launch, partly due to the timing.

Timing can interrupt a ripple movement more than any other hurdle. When the time is right, the ripple flows evenly across the lake. When the timing is wrong, a ripple is unable to progress much beyond the point of impact. An ill-timed plant can dishearten a congregation and dissuade it from planting again. People will point to the failed experience as the reason a church should never again involve itself in planting. The better the timing, the better the results; the better the results, the better the chance of parenting again.

PEACE OF MIND

My wife's phone call was terse and to the point. "You need to get home. Ryan has fallen off his scooter, and he has a gash in his arm. I can't calm him down—he needs to get to the emergency room."

Fortunately, the church was near our home so I was able to get there quickly. When I arrived, my then seven-year-old son was in our front yard in hysterics. He wanted no one near him. He knew he was hurt, but fear was the only medicine he would accept. I stepped closer and began talking to him soothingly. Once in range, I grabbed him in my arms, and he began to settle down.

Joni drove, and I sat in the passenger seat with Ryan on my lap, holding him close to my chest. I was nearly as hysterical on the inside as Ryan was on the outside, but I found the composure to calmly explain what he would soon experience in the emergency room. I told him about the registration process at the hospital. I described how we would go in a curtained room and be seated on a gurney with other sick people nearby. I explained that the doctor would give him a shot, which might hurt a little but would take away the pain. I did my best to tell him about the cleaning of the wound and the stitching of his arm. I did everything I could think of to prepare him for the experience. "You can handle this," I told him. "It's going to be all right,"

It worked. By the time we arrived at the hospital, Ryan was calm. His medical treatment went more or less as I had described, and he took it like a champ. Heightening his awareness of what was to come did much to soothe his nerves and make the entire process go smoothly.

In the same way, understanding the potential myths, hindrances, and hurdles to church parenting will demystify the process and help you to navigate it calmly and successfully. When you know what's ahead, you will be prepared to meet it. It's going to be all right. This is something you can do.

CHAPTER SEVEN

WHEN AND WHEN NOT TO PARENT

—〰—

> ## RIPPLE PRINCIPLE
> The parent church must be spiritually
> ready for church multiplication.

W hen Joni and I got married, I was only halfway through my undergraduate degree. I still had lots of schooling before me. I was facing two more years of undergraduate work and three years of graduate school. My wife and I decided not to have children until I completed my education. We felt this would be best for us relationally, economically, and professionally. Our plan worked out well. I completed my master's degree in June 1980, and our first child was born that September.

There was never any question about whether we would become parents. We knew that having children was something we wanted to do. But the timing was an issue. We wanted to provide the best possible environment for our children. Frankly, I'm not sure we were totally prepared when we had our first son, but we were more prepared than ever before.

Timing is an important consideration when parenting churches. Some times are better for parenting than others. Of course, no congregation will ever feel completely ready to become a parent church. The goal is to identify the optimum time, not the perfect time.

So how will you know when your church is ready to parent? What is the optimum time to get involved in church multiplication?[1]

POSITIVE INDICATORS

I have provided seven indicators that will help leaders identify their congregation's readiness to parent a church. These indicators have nothing to do with the number of buildings a church owns, the number of members it has, or the size of its budget. Instead, they point to the presence of the attitude and atmosphere within the church. It is not necessary to have all seven indicators in order to launch a church multiplication project. Any one of them may provide enough capital to motivate a congregation to begin the parenting journey.

A BURDEN FOR LOST PEOPLE

Any congregation that has the desire to see people brought into the Kingdom has the potential to become a parent. Church planting is the most effective method of evangelism. If a church has the heart to be a vehicle for the salvation of others, it should build church parenting into its strategic plan. Parenting is as essential a tool for winning people to Christ as are personal soul winning, door-to-door evangelism, acts of compassion, and programmed attraction events. A church that wants to reach the lost can become a parent church.

A WILLINGNESS TO STEP OUT IN FAITH

A step of faith is required to enact any vision. Many churches regularly display a willingness to do this. How do you know if a church is ready to undertake a parenting project? Has it committed surplus income to missions? Has it brought on a staff person in anticipation of growth? Have its members given above and beyond their tithes to build a building or purchase property? All of those actions are attempts to enact a vision—to make what is unseen become a reality. They are steps of faith. A church that is willing to attempt the unseen has the potential to be a parenting church.

A VISION FOR REGIONAL INFLUENCE

Earlier, I made the distinction between a regional church and a regional ministry. A regional ministry recognizes that not everyone in a given area will attend one church in one location. The largest churches in the world do not reach every person in their communities, much less in their regions. They may have outstanding programming that attracts a large number of people, but there are even more people that they will never reach.

A church that understands that concept has the potential to become a parent church. Does your congregation realize that it can multiply its effectiveness by extending its ministry beyond the property line? Does the church want to reach beyond its community (Judea) into the surrounding region (Samaria)? If so, it may be ready for church parenting.

A SPIRITUAL MATURITY

It takes mature, unselfish people to parent churches. A spiritually mature congregation is one that is growing in its understanding of the Word and its application to life. A congregation that is growing in Christ will hunger to multiply. The tug of the Spirit will draw it to spread the gospel, both individually and corporately. A church that is increasing its spiritual depth has the potential to be a parenting church.

A GENEROUS SPIRIT

A congregation that is generous toward its pastoral staff, guest speakers, missionaries, surrounding community, and neighboring churches displays a key indicator of its readiness to become a parent church. Church parenting is an act of generosity. God gives us resources so that we might be generous with them. Paul, in his letter to the Corinthian church, explains why we are to be generous. "Now he who supplies seed to the sower and bread for food will also supply and increase your store of seed and will enlarge the harvest of your righteousness. You will be *made rich* in every way so that you can be *generous on every occasion,* and through us your generosity will result in thanksgiving to God" (2 Cor. 9:10–11, emphasis added).

One of the churches I pastored had a very generous member who was a building contractor. He faithfully tithed his income, which was significant. He also gave above that, out of his God-given abundance. One time he handed me a check for $20,000. On another occasion he gave $16,000. He knew that some people had to know about his contributions, but he asked that the information loop be kept small.

As I was expressing my gratitude after he gave one significant gift, the fellow quipped, "It's just part of the deal, right? This is what we are supposed to do." He understood that those to whom God has entrusted much have an obligation to be generous. May his tribe increase, and may his attitude spill over into the local church.

A WILLINGNESS TO RISK

Every worthwhile venture carries risk, and church parenting is no different. Sometimes, that risk is the simple willingness to try, even though failure is a possibility. Has your congregation shown itself willing to take risks? Perhaps it took some risk by calling you as pastor. A church that is willing to ignore the naysayers and try something bold may be a prime candidate for church parenting.

A KINGDOM MINDSET

Ultimately, parenting churches is not about denominational survival or local church vision. It is about Kingdom expansion. A congregation that sees beyond its local or denominational affiliation and recognizes the awesome reach of the Kingdom will view church parenting as necessary. The Kingdom is expanded very little when a few churches grow larger, but it is greatly increased when churches multiply in a variety of ways.

A pastor friend once told me, "You'll never have to worry about making God mad if you try to plant a church. . . . Whatever ministry you are with, you must understand one thing: Church planting is not for us, it is for God. We do it so God will have a people to worship Him." Any church with an eye for the greater harvest field has the potential to become a parenting church.

These indicators are a foundation you can build upon as you prepare your congregation to parent churches. Which ones are already present in your people? Which might you cultivate among them?

NEGATIVE INDICATORS

There are times when parenting is not in the best interest of the parent or the potential child. When this is the case, it is better not to rush into parenthood. But how will you know that? What are the factors that indicate when it's *not* a good time to parent a church?

Here are some caution lights that should raise concern about the timing of a church parenting effort. Caution lights are not intended to halt forward progress but to raise awareness of potential danger. If your church exhibits any of these yellow lights, it may be better to make parenting a future goal.

MAJOR CHANGE

It is more difficult to complete a parenting project when the parent church is experiencing a major change. Major changes include relocation; an open or just-completed building project; pastoral transition, loss of a larger number of members due to conflict, job transfers; and a downturn in the local economy. Changes like these requiring internal adjustments in the parent church and make for less-than-ideal conditions for reproduction.

SPIRITUAL IMMATURITY

It takes an unselfish, mature congregation to parent effectively. If a congregation's spiritual temperature is low, it needs to improve its own health before assuming the responsibility of church parenting. A key indicator of immaturity is an ingrown attitude. A congregation that is always most concerned about itself is immature. Often, the result is infighting over fringe issues, such as the color of carpet for a Sunday school room, the rules for use of the kitchen, the mess the youth group leaves when it uses the fellowship hall, and whether or not to reserve parking spots for visitors and senior adults. All churches address these issues; however, if they are the focal point of board meetings, the church is not yet mature and is not in an ideal position to become a parent.

LACK OF LEADERS

In order to successfully parent a church, a congregation needs mature leaders—leaders who are *growing* forward, not *groaning* forward. Growing-forward leaders look for ways to stretch their ability and responsibility. Groaning-forward leaders are willing to take steps, but not without complaining. Which type of leaders do you have? Are they responsive to the pastor's leadership? Do they engage change easily? Or do they need to develop their understanding of effective leadership?

LACK OF REPRODUCING SYSTEMS

Churches need to have systems that model multiplication if they are to become parents. Sunday school classes and small groups should be trained to reproduce themselves. Leadership training, apprenticeships, and spiritual gift development programs also aid internal multiplication. Without internal reproduction, a congregation will be hard pressed to invest people in a daughter church project and then replace those invested.

BLURRED FOCUS

An unhealthy church may need to focus on getting healthy before attempting to parent. *Refocusing* is one tool a church can use to recover its health. Refocusing is a process by which a trained leader helps a congregation refine its sense of identity and purpose.[2] The trained leader helps first the pastor and then key leaders to align themselves with God's unique call on their lives. Ultimately, the church members walk together through steps that empower them for effective ministry. Refocusing moves a church toward health; healthy churches reproduce.

Does your church exhibit negative indicators for church parenting? Identify them, and form a plan to address them. Above all, remember that the decision to delay church parenting is not the decision to refuse it. Keep church multiplication as a future goal.

TESTING FOR READINESS

When I pastored in Vista, California, a young man served as an intern at our church for the summer. He was from the Midwest and had traveled to California by train. On the day he was to return home, my oldest son and I took him to the train depot. He had quite a bit of luggage, so we helped him stow it near his seat. While we were helping him get settled for the long journey, the train suddenly began to move. The conductor pulled up the stairs to shut the door. The train was leaving the station, and neither my son nor I wanted to go with it. I looked at the conductor and said, "I don't want to be on this train."

"Then why are you on this train?" she asked.

I explained that I was there to help a friend with his luggage, but the whole time I was thinking, *Weren't you supposed to say "All aboard!"?*

"Well, you are on the train now," the conductor deadpanned.

"Where is the next stop?" I asked, wondering if we would be traveling all the way to the Midwest.

"San Juan Capistrano," she said, then added, "Enjoy the ride."

I considered my situation. San Juan Capistrano is a small community roughly forty-five minutes north of where we lived. Since there was nothing I could do about it, I decided to enjoy the trip and call Joni to come get us in San Juan Capistrano. This changed my plans for the day, but I decided to be flexible.

Unexpected changes are always challenging, and many congregations fear the changes that church parenting will bring. Some simply aren't ready to handle it. At the beginning of any change, you must consider the situation of the church. In this chapter, I have described both positive and negative indicators of a congregation's readiness to parent a church. Evaluate your congregation with these in mind. You may also wish to use the Change Readiness Indicator instrument in Appendix B of this book to help determine your congregation's readiness to undertake church parenting. Another helpful diagnostic tool is the Church Health Survey offered online by New Church Specialties.[3] Consider your present situation, and formulate a plan that will move your congregation toward parenting. As congregational leaders participate in this evaluation, they will gain increased ownership in the vision. Remember, the issue is not whether to become involved in church parenting—but when.

CHAPTER EIGHT

LEADING A CONGREGATION INTO PARENTING

—⟋⟋⟍⟍—

> ## RIPPLE PRINCIPLE
> Ripple leaders anticipate change and
> minimize the discomfort it brings.

T he church parenting ripple begins in the heart of the pastor, but it must spread to the hearts of his or her church members. The transfer is not automatic. John Maxwell has said that most visions do not die at birth, but in transition to the congregation. The pastor must communicate the vision for parenting in language that the congregation will understand and accept. The problem, of course, is that adopting that vision will entail change. The congregation will have to accept a change in attitude about the surrounding region, the church facility, the finances, and how ministry is accomplished. And, as Mark Twain famously observed, the only person who likes change is a wet baby.

UNDERSTANDING CHANGE DYNAMICS

I travel by air regularly, and I admit that I am not a huge fan of in-flight turbulence. I feel most comfortable when the plane is moving forward, not bouncing up and down. I understand some of the factors that create turbulence, but that understanding does not increase my enthusiasm for rough spots. I do appreciate it, though, when the pilot informs the passengers that there will be some turbulence and advises them to fasten their seatbelts. That improves my confidence in the pilot. It also makes it easier to deal with the rough ride.

That *Pilot Principle* holds true for church life as well: when a leader advises followers to expect change and tells them how to deal with it, their confidence level goes up and they are more willing to continue the journey. Note that the pilot never apologizes for the turbulence — only for the inconvenience it may cause. The turbulence of change is unavoidable, but a leader can lessen the inconvenience it brings through foresight, preparation, and communication.

Some leaders seem unaware of the effects of change on their followers. That may be because leaders usually love change. After all, they initiate it! So if you have embraced the idea of church parenting, you are probably rearing to get started. You have already weighed the pros and cons. You are convinced that your church should use this method of evangelism, and you're ready to begin the adventure. But the members of your congregation are in a different position. They have just been introduced to the idea of church parenting and have not had time to process it adequately. You can expect them to be resistant.

Resistance is the initial response to any change. Congregational resistance to church parenting may come as a vague feeling that says, "I'm not sure I like this." Or it may be seen in an entrenched attitude accompanied by the tune to "We Shall Not Be Moved." But initial resistance is not the same as rejection or defiance. It is simply part of the natural process of accepting change.

Leaders are often frustrated by resistance because they expect an open-armed welcome for their new ideas. Initial resistance sometimes catches leaders like deer in the headlights—they're puzzled and unsure of what to do. *What is wrong with these people?* a leader may wonder. *Why don't they want to be led? If they were godly, they would get on board with this.*

One reason people resist church parenting is that they do not understand what it entails. Their initial resistance is a call for more information. It provides an opportunity to lead by anticipating and answering questions.

- What does it mean to parent a church?

- What impact will this have on us?

- When would we do this?

- How much will it cost?

- Do I have to go to the daughter church?

- Why do we have to get involved in this?

- Pastor, does this mean you are leaving?

The bottom line is that people want to know how a proposed change might affect them and how it will be accomplished.

When my kids were younger, they often approached me after a worship service and asked permission to do something. At what seemed to them an opportune moment, they might ask, "May we go to so-and-so's house?" Usually, I had several questions about the request but couldn't ask them because I was in the middle of a conversation with a parishioner. "Wait a few minutes," was my usual reply. Like most kids, however, mine were a little impatient and would press for a decision. Finally, I would say, "If you want my decision now, then the answer is no. But if you wait until I can think about it for a minute, the answer might be different." They were always willing to wait.

Was I resistant to their requests? Often, I was. Did that mean I rejected the idea? No, I simply had questions that needed to be answered before I could make a positive decision. When church leaders rush in with a plan and ask for an immediate decision, the congregation will resist—no matter how good the idea is. The more pressure leaders apply, the more resistance they will meet.

When you present the idea of church parenting to your people, be prepared for the turbulence it will bring. Understand the congregation's need for information, and provide it. Come with ready answers to as many questions as possible. Help people see the journey ahead and prepare for the changes it will bring. And be patient. It will take time for the church parenting ripple to spread from your heart to theirs.

MANAGING CHANGE EFFECTIVELY

Leading a major change like church parenting seems like a daunting task, but it is something that nearly every leader can accomplish by paying attention to some basics. Providing information will help a congregation embrace the idea and move toward a new course of action. From there, the following seven simple steps will minimize the turbulence of change and lead to a successful church multiplication effort. Remember this basic plan with the acronym CHANGES. (Appendix C contains an evaluation tool that may be used to implement this change management model.)

Cast a vision.

Have an end in mind.

Advance strategically.

Negotiate the problems.

Get the congregation on board.

Evaluate progress.

Show the results.

CAST A VISION

To lead a church parenting effort, you must be a vision caster. Casting the vision for church multiplication enables people to adopt goals that are outside their own perceived interests. When people own the vision for themselves, they realize that Kingdom work involves reaching people they may never see. Vision casting takes creativity because it involves rallying people to an intangible goal. It is one thing to help people see a building that is not yet built; it is quite another to help them envision a body of believers that doesn't currently exist.

The dot-com revolution brought to the fore the idea that a business does not have to be composed of brick and mortar. Move away from brick-and-mortar vision casting by opening the congregation's eyes to people and places rather than walls and roofs. Does this imply that owning property and constructing buildings are somehow contrary to church parenting? No, but it acknowledges that a different approach is required to move a congregation to create a daughter church.

HAVE AN END IN MIND

In 1990 I led a mission team to Munich, Germany. While there, an unexpected ministry opportunity presented itself when our team was invited to visit a Christian youth camp near Budapest, Hungary. We accepted the offer, loaded up two vans, and headed for the Hungarian countryside. We traveled late into the night; it was close to midnight and very dark. I was following the lead van driven by the host missionary. It appeared to me that we were wandering aimlessly through the darkened landscape, but I assumed the missionary knew where he was going.

Suddenly, the lead van pulled to the side of the road. I quickly followed suit. The missionary jumped out of his van and ran back toward the vehicle I was driving. I jumped out to meet him half way. I was concerned. Was there a problem?

"We are looking for a *buffa*," the missionary informed me. "We need to turn left at the *buffa*."

"What's a *buffa?*" I asked.

Without cracking a smile, the missionary said, "I don't know." With that he turned and ran back toward his van. Amazingly, we found the *buffa*—a small store—and arrived at our destination.

When you begin the church parenting journey, your congregation may feel that you are wandering aimlessly. It will put your people at ease if you can clearly describe your destination—the daughter church. Tell them what it will look like. Describe what a parent church should look like. Provide a biblical framework for parenting. Talk about the joy and privilege of parenting a congregation. As you point toward a clear destination, others will begin to see the value of a regional ministry. Their enthusiasm will be heightened as they catch sight of the ripples from their church reaching some distant shore.

ADVANCE STRATEGICALLY

I admire people who play chess well. It is incredible to me how they advance the pieces strategically, often planning several moves in advance. Yet when an opponent makes some unexpected move, a good player will adjust his or her response. A skilled chess player can envision the endgame well in advance and plan a strategy to achieve it.

Advancing toward the goal of church parenting requires strategic planning. To create a daughter congregation, your church will need a parent church action plan, a comprehensive blueprint for your project.[1] No action plan may be set in stone, however. Be willing to change the plan as needed. John Maxwell and Jim Dornan give this advice: "Write the goal in concrete and the plan in sand."[2] The goal is to parent a growing, healthy, reproducing church—never compromise on that. But the plan may have to be changed just as a chess player adjusts his or her strategy during a match.

Bill Dave is a layman at Arcade Wesleyan Church. He retired after thirty-five years as the civilian administrator of a large air force base in Sacramento. Bill knows what it takes to get a diverse group of people to rally around a common cause, and I adopted him as a mentor for administrative matters. At one of our coffee sessions, Bill gave me this advice, "Phil, don't ever sanctify deadlines." As parent church leaders, we can easily get caught up in deadlines. When we have declared that we will parent a church by a certain date, it becomes tempting to force the result. But the deadline is not what matters—the creation of a new, healthy, reproducing church is. If achieving that result means changing a deadline, do it. Allow the Spirit of God, not the plan, to dictate the timing.

NEGOTIATE THE PROBLEMS

As the church parenting ripple expands through your congregation, problems will arise. Anticipate them; don't ignore them. The better you anticipate problems, the better you will handle them. Here are some common challenges.

Ignorance. Some problems arise from a congregation's ignorance of church parenting. At the beginning, they know little about the process. They have not had time to consider the idea fully. That brings resistance.

The solution to ignorance is information. Provide it. Overcome the problem of ignorance by anticipating questions and answering them.

Apathy. People tend to be disinterested in those with whom they have little in common. Many church members can see little reason to reach beyond their immediate community. The solution to apathy is allegiance to the gospel message. Overcome apathy by elevating the evangelistic mission of the church.

Arrogance. A congregation that has what it needs may see no reason to help others get what they need. "We worked for our resources!" some will say. "Let new churches work for their own." The solution to arrogance is brokenness. Pray for personal and corporate brokenness over the lost. If there is not genuine brokenness in your church for unsaved people, ask God to provide it.

Distrust. It takes trust to parent a new congregation. Often, it is easier for a believer to trust God individually than for a congregation to trust him corporately. The solution to lack of trust is willing faith.

Hold the promises of God before your people along with the challenge to accept them. Take God at his word.

GET THE CONGREGATION ON BOARD

When I served on the pastoral staff of Dr. John Maxwell, he would often say, "He who thinks he is leading but has no one following is simply taking a walk." A pastor's enthusiasm for church parenting will mean nothing if the congregation does not follow. Many leaders believe they can enact their vision for church multiplication through a strong will and persistent effort—and some can. But it is a mistake to move ahead without ensuring that the congregation has ownership of the result. You want people on the ship with you, not waving good-bye from the pier. How might you accomplish that?

Work inside out. Begin with your leadership team, which might be your church board or ministry team. When these leaders catch the church parenting vision, they will help it infiltrate the congregation. Put resources into your leaders' hands. Take them to seminars on church multiplication. Share your vision with them one-on-one.

Also, communicate your vision through preaching and teaching. Preach on the biblical value of church parenting. Teach a topical series from the book of Acts. Show how the early church expanded through multiplication. Show your people that the gospel is spread through believers winning the lost to Christ and starting new churches.

Be careful to provide information in bite-sized pieces. Remember the old gag, "How do you eat an elephant? One bite at a time." It would be unwise to stand before the congregation and declare that your church will begin parenting in six months. That would be like offering them a drink of water from a fire hose. Share the vision over an extended period of time.

It may help to invite church planting leaders into your church to give their testimonies. Invite not only planting pastors but also lay people who have helped begin another church. Such testimonies will open the eyes of your people to opportunities they never knew existed.

EVALUATE PROGRESS

In the top left corner of my car's windshield there is a sticker containing several numbers. The numbers represent projected mileage. When my odometer matches those numbers, I'll know it is time to have the car's oil changed and fluids checked. This regular checkup is critical for the efficient operation of my car. Checkups are also important for managing the process of change. Schedule regular evaluation times for determining whether or not the plan is moving on schedule. Keep the desired result in mind, but be willing to change specific steps as necessary to keep the process going smoothly.

SHOW THE RESULTS

Results provide motivation. Parenting congregations must see a return on their investment or they will lose enthusiasm for church multiplication. Provide information about the daughter church—conversions, baptisms, and attendance. Invite new people from the daughter church to share the impact of Christ upon their lives. The parent church needs to see the influence it has had for God through the new congregation.

Through one of the daughter churches I've been involved with, a man renewed his relationship with Christ and began attending church again. This fellow was invited to share his testimony at the parent church one Sunday morning, and he became a living example of the unseen impact of the parent congregation. After the service, one of our members approached me and said, "Thanks for reminding me of why we do this." The results were clear.

GAINING AGREEMENT

Scripture teaches that "without a vision, the people perish" (Prov. 29:18 KJV). At one conference I attended, Sean Randall, a church planter in Sparks, Nevada, put an interesting twist on that verse. He said, "Without a people, the vision will perish." That is especially true of church parenting. A leader may begin the ripple, but unless the people participate, it will never reach the shore. One leader's vision is never enough to sustain a church multiplication movement.

As a ripple leader, you must cast the vision for church parenting among your people. There will be resistance, for no change of this magnitude is easily accepted. Remember the Pilot Principle: when a leader advises followers to expect change and tells them how to deal with it, their confidence level goes up and they are more willing to continue the journey. You are the key to managing change in your congregation. Anticipate it, prepare for it, communicate it. Don't allow the vision to perish.

CHAPTER NINE

FINANCING

CHURCH PARENTING

—⚬—

> ### RIPPLE PRINCIPLE
> Every church can finance its own multiplication
> through discipline, planning, and partnership.

S cott, my youngest son, is ready to buy his own car. He has worked out a budget and determined the monthly amount he is willing to spend on a payment. The challenge is coming up with a down payment. He knows he can make a payment of a hundred bucks or so each month, but where will he ever get the hundreds of dollars he'll need to put down? After a bit of reflection, Scott came up with his own solution. He realized that if he could afford to make a certain payment each month *after* buying the car, he could begin setting that money aside *before* the purchase. In six months or so, he will have saved enough money for a down payment.

I'm pleased that my son is learning to balance what he wants now against what he hopes to have in the future. He understands that discipline results in delight, and he has figured out that nearly any project can be affordable with careful planning and a bit of patience.

The same is true for church multiplication. Making Kingdom waves is not without cost. Parent congregations must make a significant financial investment. The funds, in most cases, must be intentionally set aside for the purpose. Yet, as Scott is learning, present planning leads to the realization of future goals. Every church can finance its own multiplication through discipline, planning, and partnership.

MORE WITH LESS

The Old Testament prophet Elisha worked many miracles. One of his greatest exploits involved an encounter with a poor widow. This often-cited story holds a great lesson for congregations that want to expand the Kingdom through church multiplication. It is found in 2 Kings 4.

One day, a widow came to Elisha. Her husband had been a prophet along with Elisha, and his death had left the woman in a difficult situation. The family owed some debts, and if she were unable to pay them, she would lose her sons to slavery. The widow had no financial resources to meet the need; she was desperate.

"What do you have in your house?" Elisha asked, a rather odd question for a destitute woman. Yet Elisha was concerned with what the woman had available to her, not what she needed. The widow's first response is typical for anyone facing an overwhelming financial challenge: "Your servant has nothing there at all." If she had had any resources, she wouldn't be facing this crisis, right? But then something clicked in her mind. No sooner had those words escaped her mouth than she remembered something that she did have—a little oil. It may have been little, but it was enough to meet her need, as Elisha soon showed her.

Established churches who contemplate church parenting often feel the same as the widow did at first. It will cost a great deal to finance a church start, and prospective parent churches usually say, "We can't afford it." Church leaders review their budgets and conclude that they don't have the financial resources to parent a congregation. Yet they neglect to consider the value of what little they do have.

Elisha instructed the widow to collect empty jars from her neighbors, then fill them with oil from her one small jar. Miraculously, her little bit of oil filled every spare jar in town, and the widow was able to sell the oil to raise money and pay her debts. A congregation's resources may seem scanty, but God can use them to help fund church parenting. Churches do not need to have an existing surplus in order to parent. With proper planning and faith, even small resources can fund a church plant.

THE BEST TIME TO BEGIN

The best time to plant a tree was twenty years ago; the next best time is now. When making financial plans for church parenting, it does no good to bemoan the fact that you didn't start earlier. It is far better to begin simply. Financial planners know this simple formula: Consistent investment plus extended time equals increased resources. The amount invested need not be large, but it must be set aside consistently. Time is the investor's ally. If your congregation has not yet begun to set money aside for church parenting, now is the time.

When I got married twenty-eight years ago, an older man pulled me aside and said, "Phil, if you wait to have children until you can afford it, you never will." At the time, his words made little sense to me. Starting a family was the furthest thing from my mind. Joni and I had been married only a month or so. I just wanted to be a husband, not a dad. As I look back, however, the advice makes perfect sense. If we had waited until we had all the money we might need before having children, we probably still wouldn't be parents. We made the best financial preparations we could—including having health insurance—but we did not wait for the "perfect time" to have kids. If your congregation waits until it can afford to parent a new church, it probably never will. It is true that your church will need a financial plan, one that includes the key coverage you'll need to become a parent. But the "perfect time" to become a parent church will never arrive.

FUNDING FROM THE PARENT CHURCH

Basketball coach Bobby Knight is credited with saying, "The will to prepare is more important than the will to win." After one of his many political defeats, Abraham Lincoln told a colleague, "I will prepare, and my time will come." Jesus said, "Suppose one of you wants to build a tower. Will he not first sit down and estimate the cost to see if he has enough money to complete it?" (Luke 14:28). The bottom line is this: you must prepare financially if you want to multiply successfully.

A parent church typically provides some financial support to its daughter. Just as married couples sometimes begin college funds for their children even before they are born, parent churches must plan ahead to meet the financial needs of their children. Here are six ways to begin making financial preparations for the birth of a daughter congregation.[1] They are not painless, but they are not overly painful. Any church with the will to multiply can finance the effort—with a little discipline.

TEACH GENEROSITY

Teach generosity to your congregation. Encourage your people to give beyond themselves. A generous church knows how to sacrifice. That church also knows the joy that comes from sharing with others. One practical way to teach generosity is to provide opportunities to give money away. Arcade Wesleyan Church began collecting an annual offering at its Christmas Eve service. This offering was given to one new church each year. The offering was announced well ahead of the service, but there was no goal amount; it was a simple freewill offering. This practice kept the goal of church parenting before the congregation, and it taught the people how to share with others.

You might develop an offering associated with a special day and have some fun with it. One church designated the Super Bowl Sunday for a special offering. Everyone was asked to bring a roll of quarters, worth ten dollars. Goal posts were constructed from PVC pipe, and with football theme music playing, people threw their quarter rolls through the uprights and into a collection basket.

PRACTICE THE 10 PERCENT RULE

Many churches have surplus funds at the end of the year. In other words, they do not spend every dollar collected. Try taking 10 percent of your church's surplus and putting it into a church planting fund. You will be amazed at the amount accrued in just a few years.

The River Church in Sacramento, California, has taken this concept to a new level. The church is not yet three years old, but from its birth, the leaders determined to give away 10 percent of the church's income. Each month, the people of River Church invest 10 percent of their tithes and offerings outside themselves. They give to support overseas missions, make gifts to the school from which they rent facilities, or support other worthwhile projects. They have even given the money to congregation members and asked them to use it to bless someone outside the church. One of these monthly gifts each year is set aside for the support of their future daughter church.

HOST A BABY SHOWER

A parent church can support a daughter church financially by sponsoring a "baby shower" for the new congregation. As with any shower, the host lists items that the new baby will need. In the case of a baby church, those would be items needed to conduct worship services, equip an office, or supply Christian education classes. Members of the parent church bring gifts to a shower, complete with cake and punch, and present them to the church planter and core team members. Wrapping the gifts can make the shower even more fun.

MAKE PARENTING A BUDGET ITEM

Include church planting as a line item in your church's annual budget. Treat it like a bill, and pay it monthly. Be as tenacious in setting aside money for this purpose as you are about paying the church's mortgage or utility bills. You could choose to make church planting part of your church's missions budget. Churches often separate domestic and foreign missions in their thinking, but both are part of the same world mission effort. Shouldn't we desire to reach those in our own communities just as much as we want to reach those around the world?

One church of about eighty people got involved in parenting by giving each year to a new church. They put church planting into their missions budget and set aside one hundred dollars per month. The pastor dreams of seeing this congregation parent a church someday. When the time comes, a financial commitment to the project has already been built into the church's financial structure.

INVEST IN OTHERS

Be willing to invest in others while you invest in yourself. One pastor wanted to incorporate preparation for church parenting into everything his congregation did. When the church needed to raise funds for a new sanctuary, it made a commitment to place 10 percent of the money received into its church parenting fund.

ESTABLISH A MEMORIAL FUND

We often see memorial funds used to finance building projects. Why not use gifts in memory or in honor of loved ones to support church parenting? When people inquire about designating memorial gifts, suggest church parenting. What better memorial could there be for a believer than a new, living church?

These few examples should do little more than get you started in devising ways to support church parenting. Creative leaders will think of dozens more. The secret is to begin preparing now, even with a small amount. A little, invested over time, will result in an abundance of resources. But you must begin. Financial preparation is a matter of will more than anything else.

FUNDING FROM THE DAUGHTER CHURCH

While my son Scott is preparing to purchase a vehicle, he is driving one of ours. We make the payments on the car, but he is responsible for all other expenses. He pays for the insurance. He buys his own gas. He covers the cost of oil changes and other maintenance. This arrangement enables him to begin driving now and makes him a financial partner in the effort. Being financially responsible helps Scott appreciate the value of the car he is driving.

Daughter churches need to be financial partners in their own start-up. If the parent church pays for everything, the daughter may fail to appreciate the cost of its existence. Starting a church works best as a cooperative venture between the new congregation, the parent church, and the denomination or association, since all three entities have a vested interest in the outcome. Here are some creative ways to involve daughter churches in their own financial health.

GET A FINANCIAL COMMITMENT FROM THE CORE GROUP

The members of your daughter church's core group will be mature Christians. It's likely that they will be people who tithe their income to your church. When they join the core team, they should be asked to make that same financial commitment to the daughter church. This core group will provide a nucleus of financial support for the church plant, and that's vital. Every daughter church must be partly responsible for its own support.

CREATE A BOOMERANG MENTALITY

When parenting a congregation, create the expectation that it will someday be responsible to invest back into the parent. When the

Arcade Wesleyan Church parented several churches, it asked each one to contribute a certain amount of money toward the parent church's future multiplication efforts. Each daughter church was asked to make this return investment within three to five years, an opportunity to which all responded enthusiastically. These "family" monies were returned within the first two years and were later used to plant more churches. This approach builds a spirit of generosity and partnership into the culture of the new church.

HAVE THE CHURCH PLANTER RAISE SUPPORT

In every church plant, the start-up pastor must raise some funds personally. This creates a sense of ownership in the project and wards off a potential welfare mentality, which expects support by every means except one's own effort.[2]

REQUIRE THE PASTOR TO BE BIVOCATIONAL

Often, new churches do not have the income to pay a full-time salary. In such cases, the planter should be willing to seek employment outside the church. Having a bivocational pastor may seem like a drawback, but it offers some advantages to a new congregation. It causes the planter to have a greater personal interest in church finances. Also, a bivocational pastor will support the church by tithing. And working in the community keeps the planter connected to the unchurched. Work relationships can yield insights into community concerns and provide witnessing opportunities.

When Keith Klassen planted Midtown Community Church in downtown Sacramento, he was committed to bridging the relational chasm between believers and non-believers. To model this commitment for his core team, Keith got a part-time job catering banquets at a private tennis club. He chose this job for several reasons. First, he had done similar work while in college. Also, it had a flexible schedule. Finally, it allowed him to work alongside the people in his target group. Several of Keith's co-workers began to attend the new church, and a few of them became Christians. In the early years of the church plant, Keith's part-time job not only provided supplemental income but also kept him out of the ministry ghetto. Every week, he was surrounded by those he hungered to reach.

A daughter church must pay something toward the salary of its pastor, and bivocational employment is not the church planter's long-term goal. Establishing an early habit of conducting budget and salary reviews will help the leadership team make a timely transition to providing full-time support for the church planter.

SEEK A PASTOR WITH OTHER INCOME

Some church planters can subsidize their own ministry through other income, particularly the support of a working spouse. When a pastor's spouse works outside the home, his or her income can free the planter to focus on starting the church. It also provides a connection to the unchurched community.

In Nampa, Idaho, the wife of a church planter worked as a fitness instructor in a local health club. She met many young mothers, and the relationships she built with them provided an open door to inviting them to church. Dozens of families came to the church as a result of this inroad.

ASK FOR DENOMINATIONAL FUNDING

It is the role of denominations to create an environment for church parenting, and that includes funding. The idea, however, is that the denomination should provide supplemental funding. The denomination should not be the sole supporter of a church plant. Here are three types of denominational funding that may be used to supplement a parenting effort.

Matching Funds. Church parenting can be encouraged when a denomination provides matching funds to parent churches. The denomination informs the parent church that a certain amount is available on a matching basis. The amount should be limited. That is, the denomination agrees to match funds up to a designated amount.

Value Added Funds. A denomination may choose to invest in a parenting effort by underscoring key values. For example, the denomination might pay for planter coaching, parent church training because it believes that these functions are essential. Or a denomination might provide health insurance or a housing allowance for the planting team to underscore the value of adequately supporting the team.

Budget Breaks. Most denominations have some system of collecting funds from their churches. This money is used to support the organization and its ministries. Generally, the assessment is not voluntary: the churches are assessed a certain annual sum based on established criteria. Denominations can provide a "break" for parent churches by temporarily reducing their financial obligation to the denomination. That not only benefits the church plant but also speeds the recovery of the parent church.

Parenting healthy reproducing churches is a team effort. Denominational structures can contribute much to create a vibrant multiplication environment.

THE PAYOFF

Is there a cost to ripple making? Absolutely, but it is a reasonable cost. With planning, persistence, and partnering with others, financing a parenting project is a reachable goal for every congregation. Now is the time to begin. Don't wait until you can afford to parent, or you may never do it. When you're tempted to think *We can't afford to parent a church,* remember instead that you can't afford *not* to.

And think of the rewards. Investments are made with the hope of a return. The return of church parenting funds is not dollars and cents. The return is a multiplication of the Kingdom. The dollars we invest do not merely buy brick and mortar. They establish new, healthy, reproducing churches—churches that will add souls to the Kingdom for years to come. Isn't that an investment worth making?

CHAPTER TEN

BUILDING A
PARENTING TEAM

—ɷ—

It had been one of those long days that pastors sometimes experience. I had gone to church early that morning and had appointments into the evening. I was leading a Bible study that night, so I didn't go home for dinner. Finally, after our evening programs were concluded, I waved good-bye to the technicians who were tinkering with the sound system and headed home. I was looking forward to putting my feet up and having a Pepsi and a bowl of popcorn as my wife, Joni, and I watched one of our favorite television programs.

When I entered the house, Joni asked, "Where's Megan?" Megan is our daughter, who was eleven years old at the time.

"I don't know." I said. "I thought she was with you." The look on Joni's face told me that I thought wrong.

"I left her at church," she said. "She was going to come home with you." The tone of my lovely wife's voice let me know there would be no discussion as to who would go back and get Megan. Joni and I had both made an assumption. Each of us thought the other would be responsible for looking after our daughter. As a result, no one took responsibility until there was a problem.

The same thing can happen in parent churches. The pastor and the laity may both assume that someone else is responsible to lead the parenting effort. Laypeople may think the pastor will head up the project while the pastor believes it's the congregation's responsibility. As a result, the parenting process never begins or, worse yet, stalls soon after starting. The ripple will never reach the water's edge unless pastors and laypersons take mutual responsibility for church parenting. It takes a team to plant a church.

During my senior year in high school, I played on a football team that won its league championship. That achievement would have seemed farfetched during my first two years of high school competition. During those years, our team's record was 0-17-1. That's zero wins, one tie, and seventeen losses! The tie occurred in the first game I played in high school. Little did I know that that tie would be the highlight of my first two seasons.

During my junior year, everything changed. Players started practicing harder. We gained skill. We began to play better, and we began to win. By the end of my senior year, we had become champions. What happened? We got a new head coach, Dwight Morris; he made all the difference. Coach Morris knew that the secret to success in football is to form a group of *individuals* into a *team*. And he understood the components needed to build a winning team: the right players, good preparation, a purpose, and a plan. When the right people come together for the right purpose, anything is possible.

That's why churches are planted most effectively by purpose-driven teams. Ministry teams always trump committees. The very word *committee* conjures the image of a slow moving, visionless, and stodgy group of people. This is a bit overstated, perhaps, but committees seldom inspire progress and innovation. Committees are focused on process. The word *team*, on the other hand, implies action and purpose. Teams are focused on a goal, and they discover methods to reach it.

It's vital to assemble a team for creating a reproducing church. This parenting team is brought together for a purpose, then disbanded when the mission is accomplished. If a church parents regularly, a new team can be assembled for each new plant. Doing so will involve more people in the process, and the more people that are involved, the greater will be the sense of ownership within the congregation.

There are three essential partnerships in successful church parenting: congregational partnerships, planter partnerships, and denominational partnerships. Each has a contribution to make. This chapter focuses on congregational partnership, and the following two chapters discuss planter and denominational partnerships. Here are the steps to building a winning church parenting team.

DETERMINE THE COMPOSITION OF THE TEAM

Coach Morris inherited a group of players, but he wasn't obligated to use them. He knew the kind of players he was looking for: guys who were willing to sacrifice for the team. He wanted individuals who would build one another up, not tear one other down. One of his first tasks was to select players who had the right attitude.

When putting together a team that will take the ripple to the water's edge, look for players who have the right stuff. You want a team that is well led and displays the right characteristics.

MEMBER CHARACTERISTICS

Teamwork. Team members must affirm the value of teamwork over individual accomplishment. They must be willing to work together. If they view themselves as a collection of individuals instead of a unified core, there will be conflict.

Commitment. Team members must be sold on the idea of church parenting and be fully committed to it. Placing people on the team will not convince them of the need to parent. You will want only those who are already convinced to serve there.

Evangelistic Zeal. To serve effectively on a parenting team, members must believe in evangelism. They must further believe that church planting is the most effective method of evangelism. Evangelistic thinkers will have a passion to build the Kingdom by planting new churches.

Optimism. Parenting is a challenging endeavor, so you do not want naysayers on your team. Recruit people who can find the opportunity in every obstacle.

Faith. Team members must be people of faith. They must be willing to believe God for the impossible. Parenting team members must embrace a vision of what a parenting congregation looks like. They must be able to look beyond what is seen into the unseen. That takes faith.

MEMBER GIFTS

In addition to these characteristics, which you will want in every person on the team, you'll want to see specific gifts displayed by various members.

Strategic Thinking. You will need at least one strategic thinker, someone who is adept at reasoning through a process. This person understands goals, objectives, plans, and strategic steps. Strategic thinkers typically ask penetrating questions.

Institutional Memory. A church historian makes a helpful team member. He or she knows the personality and dynamics of your congregation and can give you a sense of where it has been spiritually and emotionally. A historian helps the team avoid repeating mistakes. A long-tenured pastor is likely such a person.

Ministry Involvement. People who are active in the church's ministry will contribute greatly to the team's effectiveness. You do not need to have every Sunday school class, interest group, or ministry represented. This would make a cumbersome team. Determine which groups are most critical to the success of the parenting effort and involve them.

Creative Thinking. Creative thinkers are an asset to a parenting team. Church parenting is not a conservative endeavor. You want people who see things a bit off center. They will stretch the team, forcing others to break free from the confines of conventional wisdom. Often, free thinkers will irritate others with their unique way of viewing the parenting process. That creative tension will force the team to consider new options and think clearly about the choices it makes.

TEAM LEADERSHIP

I am frequently asked, Who should lead the team? The leader should be a significant member of the parent church's pastoral staff, ideally the senior pastor. If he or she is unable to function in this role, a highly regarded staff member should lead. The status of the team leader communicates importance of parenting to the congregation.

In Olathe, Kansas, a large Nazarene church is active in parenting new congregations. The senior pastor chose not to lead the team, but he assigned leadership to the executive pastor. That sends a clear message to the congregation. The executive pastor's leading role communicates that church parenting is a significant emphasis of the church.

TEAM SIZE

How many members should serve on a church parenting team? This is left to the discretion of the pastoral leaders. Guard against the team becoming too cumbersome and unmanageable. A lean team is an effective team. Eight to twelve members, not including the team leader or pastoral staff members, is usually an ideal number.

CAREFULLY RECRUIT TEAM MEMBERS

When you have an idea of the desired composition of the team, you can begin recruiting. Team selection begins with prayer. Before you recruit your parenting team, recruit a small intercessory team to support it. The intercessors' role is to pray for the team members, for openness in the hearts of congregation members, for the church planter, and for the spiritual preparation of potential planting locations. Prayer is the backbone of the parenting process.

Next, develop a ministry description for parent team members. This description should include key expectations, responsibilities, and time commitments. (A sample Planting Team Ministry Description can be found in Appendix D.)

Then, ask key church leaders to suggest potential parent team members. Poll board members, small group leaders, Sunday school teachers, and other leaders. Share the team's ministry description with them, and ask them to suggest the names of people who would be a good fit. Prayerfully pare the list to a manageable number. Remove from consideration anyone who does not meet the team criteria. When you have reduced the list to two or three names more than your goal number of participants, you're ready to recruit.

The next step is to meet individually with potential members. Meeting face-to-face for coffee or a meal emphasizes to your prospective teammates the importance of the parenting project. When you meet, share the team's vision and ministry description with them, and review your expectations for each person serving on this team. Allow an opportunity to ask questions. Do not press potential team members for their commitment at the conclusion of this meeting; you do not want a premature response, either yes or no. Candidates need time, probably a week, to prayerfully consider their involvement. Follow up this meeting with a phone call—don't ask them to call you.

Coach Morris knew that if his players were in good physical condition, they could begin working sooner on offensive and defensive plans. The better prepared your team is, the sooner it can begin the actual work of planning the parenting project. Once the team is in place, call its first meeting within two weeks. The sooner you begin planning, the sooner the dream of parenting will come to fruition.

OUTLINE THE TEAM'S PURPOSE

I can still remember our first team meeting with Coach Morris. He told us that our purpose was twofold: work hard and win a championship. He summed it up with these words: "The team that wins in this league is the team that works the hardest. No team will work harder than we will." If nothing else, we knew what lay ahead of us that year; we knew our purpose.

The parenting team's purpose is simple: develop a plan for the effective parenting of a healthy, reproducing church. The purpose is not to make a plan for the actual *planting* of the church. The planter is responsible for those details. The parenting team is to devise a plan that will put in place the elements needed to *parent* a church.

Parent church teams often get caught up in the wrong aspect of planning. They think it is their responsibility to determine the location, target audience, and the steps needed to start the church. That isn't their job. The parenting team is responsible to prepare the parent congregation for church planting. The team leader must clearly identify that purpose for the team and keep it working toward that goal. The parenting team will be responsible for at least the following actions.

- Identify and recruit intercessors who will pray for the parenting project.

- Communicate a biblical understanding of parenting to the congregation.

- Develop a biblical understanding of the directive to parent.

- Create awareness of the process of change that awaits the congregation.

- Clarify relationships and mutual expectations with denominational leaders and with the planting pastor.

- Create a timeline for the project and identify critical milestones.

DEVELOP A PARENTING PLAN

Seldom do churches just spring into existence. Healthy churches result from proper planning and implementation. Your team will need to crystallize its dream into a clear action plan. In high school, Coach Morris devised offensive and defensive plans for our team. Coach approached this task with an interesting philosophy. Instead of presenting a preselected offensive strategy and trying to make the players implement it, he evaluated the talent of the team and designed his offensive strategy accordingly. The plays we used were designed to fit the players, not vice versa.

That is exactly the way a church parenting team should devise its action plan. Begin by evaluating the congregation; each one is different. A plan that works for one may not be suitable for another. A workable parenting plan ought to include five key actions.

CHOOSE A MODEL

First, determine the parenting model that you will use. Review the intentional parenting models listed in chapter four. In light of your congregation's strengths, abilities, and attitudes, which model would work best for you?

SET EXPECTATIONS

Second, set expectations for the parenting project. We all have expectations about our involvement in a given endeavor and the results it will bring. Miscommunicating or not communicating those expectations can result in frustration and misunderstanding.

I once coached a church planter in western Canada. During our first meeting, I discovered that he was frustrated by uneasiness between him and the officials of his denomination. As we discussed the matter, it became clear that neither party had laid down clear expectations. The planter believed that he was right on track, planting a wonderful church. Yet the denomination's leaders believed the project—and their investment—had gone awry. Each party was working from a different set of expectations. The parenting team can avoid this trap by devising clear expectations and communicating them to the parent congregation, the daughter church, and the denomination.

Expectations for the Parent Church. When determining expectations, consider the following questions: What can the daughter church expect from the parent? What resources will be made available? How long will the parent invest in the daughter?

A key principle is that the parent should *under promise* and *over deliver.* For example, if the parent church promises $5,000 in support but is able to invest $10,000, the daughter congregation is overjoyed. Now reverse that situation. If the parent church promises $10,000 but is able to provide only $5,000, the daughter church may feel betrayed.

The daughter church should expect that support will not be cut off immediately after birth. Parent congregations sometimes cut off the new church financially, emotionally, or organizationally too soon. An infant congregation may not survive alone. An effective parenting plan will allow adequate time for the new church to stabilize. The amount of time will vary depending on the size of the core team and the up-front financial investment of the parent. The parent congregation should clarify the length of time that the daughter can count on receiving support. However, it may be necessary to be flexible in light of the current situation when that deadline arrives.

On the other hand, the parent should avoid becoming an overbearing presence in the life of its child. There are times when a parent church will not allow the new church to grow. Layers of expectation are placed on the daughter, which result in keeping the new church dependent on the parent for too long. The action plan must foresee cutting the apron strings and letting the daughter church become responsible for herself.

Expectations for Others. There will be expectations, stated or unstated, for other parties in the church planting effort. The daughter church, the planting pastor, and the parenting pastor each have responsibilities. It is best to clarify them at the beginning of the project, then communicate them to everyone involved.

What can the parent expect from the daughter? When will the daughter be self-sufficient? What communication should come from the daughter? What kind of reporting is expected, and how frequently should it be made?

What is expected of the parent church pastor? He or she must give people permission to go with the planter. No one but the senior pastor can do this. The parent church pastor must also provide the planter with some exposure to the congregation and allow him or her to recruit core team members. That exposure might take the form of preaching opportunities, teaching Sunday school classes, or anything that will cast the planter in a positive light.

What is expected of the daughter church pastor? One of the biggest errors in church planting is having the right place but the wrong planter. As the parenting team selects a planter, it must seek an individual who will fit into the potential planting communities and who shares the philosophy of church multiplication. When parenting congregations, I was never interested in working with a planter who wanted to plant only one church. We were starting a multiplication movement, not planting a solitary church; therefore, we looked for planters who wanted to plant reproducing churches and become parent pastors themselves someday.

Also, the planter must be loyal to the parent church pastor. The planter cannot express a sense of competitiveness or one-upmanship toward the parent pastor. And the planter is responsible to grant permission for people to remain at the parent church. He or she must not make people feel like second-class believers because they do not sense a call to the church plant. The planter must present the new church as an extension of the vision of the parent church. The new church must not be seen as a means of finally "doing church right."

ARRANGE FINANCING

Third, determine a plan for financing the church plant. There are many ways to underwrite the planting of a new church. Review the ideas for financing a church parenting effort in chapter nine, and determine which method or methods best suits your situation.

ESTABLISH RECRUITING METHODS

Fourth, the action plan must address the manner in which core team members will be recruited for the daughter church. Without careful communication, recruitment can be a quagmire. The parenting team must establish guidelines that allow a planter to recruit members from the parent congregation. In the parenting endeavors I have led, we gave our planters two instructions: (1) Anyone may be recruited except for staff members, and (2) recruiting must be done only within a designated five-month timeframe. These guidelines worked well for us. You will need to develop guidelines that work for you and your congregation.

PLAN FOR RECOVERY

Finally, the parenting team must include an action plan for recovering from the parenting effort. My biggest mistake in parenting, by far, was not giving the parent church enough time to recover. I underestimated the impact the birth of a new church would have on the parent congregation, and I underestimated the impact it would have on me. Just as many new moms experience postpartum blues, many parent churches experience post-planting blues. These blues are the sense of loss felt by the parent congregation and pastor. The parenting team should prepare for this and make a plan to deal with it. The parent church needs some R & R—recovery and rejuvenation—after giving birth. Expect it, and plan for it.

Developing an action plan may not come naturally to the parenting team members. It is wise to arrange for some training on how to develop a plan. Consider enlisting a coach to help the parent church team through this process. Someone who has led his or her congregation through a parenting process would be an ideal coach. And remember that the plan must not be stagnant; it must be flexible to meet changing circumstances within the congregation.*

CATAPULTING THE DREAM INTO A MOVEMENT

Catapulting a parenting dream into a movement is the destiny to which Kingdom-conscious leaders should aspire. Creating a movement will take plenty of heart—the heart to regularly participate in church parenting endeavors, the heart to take more and more territory for God by creating reproducing churches, the heart to recruit other church leaders to join in sending ripples to the other shore. Between each planting effort, there will be a recovery time. But never allow your congregation to lose sight of the vision for church multiplication. Most healthy churches can and should reproduce every three to four years. By doing so, we ensure that our legacy will outlive us. The churches we help parent will become living monuments to the grace of God in the lives of people. Do not fall short of the incredible plan God has for his church.

The parenting team is a critical component in church multiplication. I have heard it said that individuals win trophies, but teams win championships. That is doubly true for church multiplication. Build your team to win. Send the ripple all the way to the water's edge.

CHAPTER ELEVEN

THE PLANTER AND HIS OR HER CORE TEAM

—ɯ—

RIPPLE PRINCIPLE
The right plan will fail without the right leader.

There is no substitute for leadership. That's why the planter selection is so important to the success of a church parenting effort. The church planter will be the pastoral leader of the fledgling congregation. The planter's leadership can make or break a new church. Having the right plan in the right place with the wrong planter is a formula for failure. Planter selection is a critical step in the parenting process. It is also an excellent opportunity for a local church and its denomination to work in partnership.

The denomination can provide a bullpen of church planters, pastors who are ready to step up and take the lead in a planting project. That involves recruiting, assessing, and training pastors for the role of church planter. But congregations know the local territory best. Local leaders understand the requirements of a particular assignment and have a better feel for the mix of capabilities and temperament that it requires. That's why the parent church should make the final selection of the planter. Working together, the parent church and denomination can find the best candidate for any given church planting situation.

SELECTING THE PLANTER

Potential planters are everywhere. Youth pastors, assistant pastors from larger churches, senior pastors of growing churches, and lay persons seeking to enter the ministry may all be good candidates. Successful church planters may come from a variety of educational backgrounds, theological perspectives, and experiences. Most, however, will display two prominent traits: a passion for lost people and an entrepreneurial spirit.

Dr. Charles Ridley has done extensive research on the characteristics of a successful church planter. Based on hundreds of interviews with planting pastors, Ridley has identified thirteen attributes commonly displayed by successful planters.[1] According to Ridley, a good church planter will display thirteen essential characteristics:

- Vision

- Intrinsic motivation

- Commitment to creating congregational ownership of ministry

- Ability to relate well to the unchurched

- Cooperation with his or her spouse

- Effectiveness at building relationships

- Commitment to church growth

- Responsiveness to the community

- Willingness to make use of others' gifts

- Flexibility and adaptability

- Ability to build group cohesiveness

- Resilience

- Ability to exercise faith

These characteristics have become the standard for church planter recruitment and assessment. A planter should not be placed in the field unless he or she has gone through an extensive assessment process. Appendix E contains a church planter self-inventory based on Ridley's thirteen characteristics. Other forms of assessment include personality inventories, interviews, and simulation exercises that measure team building, problem solving, or other aspects of church planting. A married church planter should never be assessed apart from his or her spouse. If the spouse is not fully committed to the dream, the project may be quickly derailed. Assessment of the planting couple ensures that both are willing to pursue this dream as a team.

Careful assessment of a prospective church planter is the best up-front investment of funds a church can make. Thousands of dollars may be saved by determining the planter's suitability for an assignment before committing funds to his or her support.[2]

TRAINING THE PLANTER

Once selected, a church planter needs to be trained. Church planting requires several competencies that are not necessarily within the portfolio of a senior pastor or staff member at an established church. Offering training to the planter allows him or her to learn the key components of launching a new church. The training team typically comprises men and women who have had hands-on experience in starting a new church.[3]

During the training phase, the church planter must acquire the tools to develop a church planting action plan. The plan should include these elements:

- The church planter's vision

- A strategy for building an intercessory team

- A timeline that begins when the planter arrives at the parent church and continues through the launch of the new church

- A ministry flow chart that shows how the planter will guide new believers to becoming fully functioning followers of Jesus Christ

- A budget for the daughter church

- A plan for developing a core team

- Plans for the daughter church's first public worship

This plan will become the planter's blueprint. The planter should present it to the leaders of the parent church, who can help refine the plan. It is the parent church's responsibility to provide the planter with an environment to enact his or her plan.

It is essential for the planter to have a coach who will ask challenging questions and keep him or her on track when drawing up the church planting plan. The coach also provides encouragement, a listening ear, and accountability. A parent church should not allow a planter to proceed without a qualified coach to walk alongside him or her.

A qualified coach is someone who both understands the church planting process and has received training on coaching methods. A coach need not have been a church planter. Many times, former planters simply coach others to plant as they did. Often, the best coaches are pastors of growing churches. These leaders understand the growth process and can help the planter be effective within the confines of his or her ability. Successful pastors also understand church organization and structure, an area in which church planters do not always excel.

It is recommended that the parent pastor *not* act as the coach. The parent church pastor needs to invest energy in the parenting congregation; coaching the planter distracts from this. The parent pastor can best serve the planter by making sure the parenting congregation invests all it can in the success of the new church. Also, a parent pastor may unintentionally become protective of the parent church and hold the planter back. Another person serving as coach may be more objective and better able to balance the needs of the mother and daughter churches.

RECRUITING THE CORE TEAM

The planter will become the leader of the new congregation, but he or she will not act alone. The planter must be surrounded by a solid *core team*, members of the parent congregation who form the nucleus of the daughter church.

The planter and the parent pastor should communicate about recruiting potential core team members. Guidelines for recruiting will already have been determined by the parenting team. The planter will need to know whom he or she can recruit, when the recruitment period begins and ends, and any other guidelines the parent church has determined. The planter, by agreement with the parent pastor, should develop a covenant for core team members to sign, which states the planter's expectations. (A sample Core Team Covenant is provided in Appendix F.) A person is considered part of the core team when he or she has signed the covenant and been approved by the planting pastor.

Some planters insist that core team volunteers should commit themselves to supporting the daughter church for an indefinite time—that is, forever. That is usually counterproductive. A better approach is to ask for a one-year commitment. That way, being part of the core team is seen as a short-term mission assignment, not a permanent separation from the mother church. Most people, however, do not return to the parent church after one year. Having taken ownership of the new church's vision, they usually choose to stay with it. Church planter Jim Bogear recruited core team members by telling them, "Commit for a year, then leave if you can." Most recruits couldn't leave when the year was up. They had become too attached to the daughter congregation.

The parent pastor plays an essential role in core team recruiting by giving congregation members permission to go with the daughter church. The parent pastor must have the attitude of John the Baptist, who encouraged his followers to go and follow Jesus. I believe John the Baptist provided Jesus with the core team for his ministry. According to John 1:29–37, John did three things that empowered his followers to follow Jesus.

First, John shifted attention to Jesus. Seeing Jesus coming, John declared him to be the Lamb of God, the one about whom John had been prophesying. This not only caught the attention of John's followers but also freed them to consider following Jesus. In much the same way, parent pastors must shift attention to the planter. Failure to do so will undermine the congregation's openness to being recruited.

Second, John gave Jesus credibility. That credibility came in the form of John's personal testimony about Jesus. Parent pastors give credibility to church planters. This is why it is imperative for the parent pastor, together with the church's leaders, to have final say in selecting the planter. The parent pastor must be able to convincingly recommend that person to the congregation.

Third, John released his followers to go with Jesus by refraining from calling them back when they made the choice to follow Jesus. Only the parent pastor can give his or her congregants permission to go. Such permission provides the planter with ideal recruiting conditions.

The parent pastor must also ensure that the congregation receives consistent communication about the progress of core team recruitment. Praying for the planter and the core team should be a regular part of public worship. The planter must be given opportunities to address the congregation in more than a cursory way. The planter should have a role in promoting the parenting plan and communicating its progress.

One of Arcade Wesleyan Church's daughter pastors had great musical skill and so was active in the church's music ministry. That kept him before the congregation every week and clearly showcased his strengths. Another of Arcade's planting pastors had experience in working with college-aged people, so he was given prominent ministry roles with that segment of the congregation. Giving important ministry assignments to the church planter enhances his or her image and credibility.

Successful recruitment depends upon clear communication between the parent pastor, planting pastor, and parent congregation. Each plays a critical role in recruiting planting core members. They are like legs of a three-legged stool. If any one leg is missing, the stool will be unstable. All three must be involved in the recruiting effort.

COMMISSIONING THE PLANTER AND CORE TEAM

Commissioning the planter and core team is the apex of the parenting process. This is the moment when the core team is released to begin a new work. An entire service should be built around this celebration. (See Appendix G for a Commissioning Liturgy.) Make the music uplifting, and emphasize the Great Commission in the sermon. Bring the entire core team in front of the congregation for a laying on of hands by the church's leaders. If the parent church conducts multiple services, repeat the act of commissioning. If the parenting effort is being made by more than one congregation, a commissioning should be held at each parent church. The act of commissioning is a high day in the life of the parent church; it is impossible to go over the top with it. No level of excitement is too high. No joy is greater. Break out the balloons. Hang banners. Throw confetti. This send off will become a highlight in the memory of your church.

During Arcade's first commissioning of a daughter church, we invited the core team to the front of the church to be presented to the congregation. Surprisingly, a couple who lived in the area of the plant but had shown minimal interest in the new church came forward with the team. I whispered to the church planter, "Did you know Chuck and Shirley were going with you?" He smiled broadly, "I had no idea, but it looks like they are." This couple became key players in the life of the new church. The excitement generated by the commissioning service is what drew them into the project.

Remember that the sending service is a party celebrating new life, not a wake mourning lost members. There will be some sadness as friends and family members leave the mother church, but the result will be a new community of changed lives. What could be more exciting?

Midtown Community Church is a daughter of Arcade Wesleyan. It began in July of 1998 in the living room of the founding pastor, Keith Klassen. Twelve people gathered on that first Sunday. Since then, Midtown has grown significantly and had a great impact in its corner of downtown Sacramento. What is that worth? Here is the value of that church, told in the words of Desiree, one of its first converts.

> The door was now open, but I still hadn't asked [Jesus] in. It wasn't until Keith's sermon on foundations that I examined my own and realized that I hated the person I had become. That night, I threw myself at the Lord's feet and begged for his mercy and forgiveness; I had finally invited him in. Since that day, my life has changed. He's taken the hate and anger that used to burn inside me and replaced it with peace, joy, and love. With God, I'm learning what real love is all about.

It is Desiree and the thousands like her that we celebrate when a core team is commissioned. The daughter church will reach people whom the parent would never touch. Lives will be changed because a church dared enough to care and invest its best for Kingdom purposes.

Now that is a reason to celebrate!

CHAPTER TWELVE

WORKING WITH A DENOMINATION

—⟋∽⟍—

> ## RIPPLE PRINCIPLE
> Denominations provide the environment
> in which churches can multiply.

A s parents, Joni and I have an overwhelming concern for the
health and well-being of our children. Since before they were
born, we have done all we could to provide a proper home for them.
We want them to be safe, secure, well fed, educated, and even disci-
plined when necessary. Why? We want them to grow into healthy,
mature adults. As their parents, it is our responsibility to give them a
home, a place where they can thrive.

In the same way, denominations create an atmosphere in which
local churches can grow, mature, and eventually become parents
themselves. Church multiplication is the responsibility of the local
church. Yet denominations or associations provide the support
without which a church parenting movement cannot thrive. These
sponsoring bodies empower the local church to multiply by providing an environment where the ripple principle can be put into
practice.

Unfortunately, local churches and their supporting institutions often see themselves as adversaries, not partners, in the parenting process. But if the ripple of church multiplication is to spread, local churches and denominations must learn to work together.

WORKING TOGETHER

When supporting a church planting movement, one challenge for a denomination is to allow appropriate freedom to the local church. Denominations often withdraw their support when they sense that they have "lost control" of a planting situation. The local church, on the other hand, may view itself as a lone ranger, valiantly struggling to right the wrongs of its denomination.

No local church can afford to be a renegade. A local church that uses a church plant to "fix" its denomination has missed the point. The object of a church plant is to redeem the lost, not reform denominational culture. The goal is to cooperate with, not compete with, the denomination and its leaders.

Neither should the denomination or association think of itself as the keeper of the torch. The energy for church planting does not emanate from a headquarters building; it pulsates from the local church; therefore, the local church must have control over any planting situation. Such decentralization of authority may be unfamiliar and even threatening to classic corporate structures. As a result, administrative leaders may be tempted to protect the fortress rather than supply the troops.

Part of the problem is that the local church and its sponsoring agency approach church planting from different perspectives. But both entities are needed. Parenting is not a solo mission. The role of each organization should be clearly identified and spelled out in the parenting plan. Local leaders are responsible to understand the denomination's structure and how it functions. That organizational system will provide resources for the local church, including a historical framework, prayer warriors, funding, skilled coaching, discipleship materials, and a place to recruit church planters. A solid partnership between the local church and its governing body will provide accountability, encouragement, and resources for the mission.

When drafting a parenting plan, a local church should consider these questions about partnering with its denomination.

- Who are the key leaders in the organization?

- What communication systems can I use to keep denominational leaders adequately informed?

- Do we need permission to parent?

- What resources can the denomination make available to us?

- How can we gain access to those resources?

- What are the formal organizational expectations for local churches?

- What are the informal organizational expectations (unspoken rules) for local churches?

Finding the answers to those questions will lead to an effective partnership between the local church and its denomination, one that is more concerned about getting results than taking credit.

LAYING THE FOUNDATION

Denominations and associations of churches have a vested interest in serving as a catalyst for church parenting. Their future depends upon creating a positive environment for church multiplication. The survival of any denomination or association whose primary goal is to create *larger* churches will always be in doubt. The denomination that creates *more* churches will thrive.

In order for a denomination to foster church multiplication, it must have a solid foundation for church planting. That foundation is composed of four elements: historical perspective, relational accountability, biblical integrity, missiological clarity.

HISTORICAL PERSPECTIVE

Before it can address the issue of church parenting, a denomination must discover the answer to this question: Where have we been? It must come to understand its own history with regard to starting new churches. Church leaders who try to initiate a church planting movement but ignore their denomination's unique story will certainly face resistance. Such leaders may be perceived as invalidating a rich heritage, and others may be slow to buy in to their fresh approach. Before initiating a church planting movement, a leader should seek the answers to these questions.

- Why did the denomination plant churches in the past?
- When, where, and how did it plant them?
- Who were the church planters?
- How did the denomination motivate and support planting?
- How did it fund planting?

Answers to these questions will form a historical perspective from which to expand a planting movement.

RELATIONAL ACCOUNTABILITY

The church is not an institution; it is a people. Consequently, relationships in the church are of paramount importance. A movement devoid of relational ties will quickly disintegrate. Relational accountability must be built into any church multiplication movement.

I liken this relational accountability to a river and its banks. The river itself represents those who are pushing for multiplication to happen. Their energy flows from a source and is directed toward a goal. The riverbanks, which guide the river, represent accountability structures. The river is given freedom to move, but not to overflow its banks. A river without banks is unpredictable and dangerous.

Banks without a river are dry and useless. The river and its banks complement one another.

Likewise, accountability between planters and denominational leaders is critical. Building strong *relational* accountability—as opposed to mere organizational compliance—will keep the multiplication effort flowing in the right direction. Relational accountability creates loyalty. Organizational compliance can foster an attitude of rebellion. This attitude may be expressed by an unwillingness to communicate. John Beilein, the head basketball coach at West Virginia University, summarized this dynamic succinctly when he said, "Rules without relationships equals rebellion."[1]

Denominations sometimes unintentionally slow down the momentum of a parenting effort by imposing too many layers of accountability. The denomination may operate under unrealistic timelines, impose cumbersome reporting systems, stipulate a single methodology, or be unwilling to transfer authority to the local church. The challenge for denominations is to determine which accountability systems need to be in place and present them in a way that makes local leaders feel that they are part of a team, not cogs in an institutional wheel. When church planters believe that their efforts merely serve the organizational structure, accountability measures will hold little, if any, value for them.

BIBLICAL INTEGRITY

The third foundational element for a planting movement is biblical integrity. Church multiplication is biblical. It is the method God has used and will use to expand his Kingdom around the world. When a denomination or association commits to church multiplication, it must do so with the conviction that planting is the continuation of Christ's command to "go and make disciples" (Matt. 28:19–20). There is no other valid motive for church planting. Denominations need to insure that church multiplication remains firmly established within a scriptural framework.

A denomination's ecclesiology will influence the approach it takes to church multiplication. The church is central in fulfilling God's purpose in the world, and local congregations are the context in which people are saved and nurtured in the faith. Therefore, denominations have a responsibility to inform congregations of the biblical mandate to multiply and to include them in church planting efforts. There are many valid multiplication methods, but none should be allowed to violate the integrity of the biblical mission.

Acts 15 provides an example of the role of organizational leaders in ensuring the integrity of a movement. The Jerusalem Council was convened to clarify and provide credibility to the early multiplication movement among the Gentiles. The Council's role was not to confine the movement but to confirm it within a biblical structure. As Tim Chester observes, "Church planting is an opportunity to reinvent church along radical biblical lines."[2] Denominations help to maintain the biblical integrity of a church planting movement.

MISSIOLOGICAL CLARITY

Clarity of mission is the fourth element in a solid foundation for church parenting. Denominations and organizations need to know where they are going. Movement without clarity often results in maintenance. Without a definite sense of direction, an organization begins to look for ways to get by instead of ways to take more ground.

Living in Sacramento, I am an avid fan of our professional basketball team, the Kings. Although I love to watch them play, it can be frustrating at times. Sometimes the team builds a significant lead in the first three quarters of the game, only to see it dwindle away before the buzzer. The players stop pushing the ball up the court. They begin to take quick shots instead of passing for the best shot. To put it simply, they become content. Occasionally, that costs them the game.

That can happen to organizations also. When they lose focus on the mission, they stop doing the things that once helped them multiply. They forget that church planting is a team effort. They relax instead of continuing to develop. The antidote to that complacency is to refocus on the mission. When a denomination remembers the mandate to "go and make disciples," it will be interested in multiplying churches.

DEVELOPING FLEXIBLE STRUCTURES

San Francisco's Golden Gate Bridge is an engineering marvel. The 9,266-foot suspension bridge is an example of *complementary contrast*. It is both flexible and foundational. It rests on pillars, driven deep into the ocean floor. These pillars provide structural stability. Yet above ground, the bridge's superstructure is flexible, designed to withstand high winds and earthquakes. In order to be effective at church parenting, denominations, too, must display complementary contrast. They must have both stable foundations and flexible super-structures, which can meet the demands of an ever-changing world.

How can we develop such denominations? Here are six suggestions.

RAISE UP VISIONARY LEADERS

Visionary leadership will create solid yet flexible denominations. Visionaries see the new day. Visionary leaders lead people toward a goal that is as yet unseen. Leaders with vision force an organization to move forward. Does your denomination have anyone who casts a vision for church multiplication? If not, who might step forward to provide that visionary leadership?

ALLOW STRUCTURES TO EBB AND FLOW

Rigid structures force every church planting situation into the same, predictable mold. Ebb and flow structures reflect the organiza-tion's ability to adapt to a new situation rather than forcing the move-ment into existing systems.

The rain and snowmelt from northern California, where I live, help supply water for the entire state of California. That water can be transported in two ways. One is via aqueduct. An aqueduct is a pipeline that moves the water decisively forward over a fixed path. It is a no-nonsense approach: direct and quick. A river moves water in a more relaxed manner. It ebbs and flows, taking the scenic route to its destination. Both systems deliver water. One adapts to the landscape, and the other ignores it. Effective denominations prefer ebb and flow structures. They nurture multiplication by adapting to a variety of methods for creating new churches.

PROMOTE SUCCESS AT EVERY LEVEL

Denominations that are most successful in creating an environment for church parenting are those that promote success at every level of the organization. Denominations can foster church multiplication by creating opportunities for churches of all sizes and planters of all abilities to participate and be affirmed. When they do, they display a Dean Witter attitude, which measures success "one investor at a time." Healthy, growing denominations consider the unique potential of one church, one planter, one community, one idea, and one opportunity at a time; they are eager to see every church succeed in making a ripple for the Kingdom.

CREATE A FAMILY REUNION MENTALITY

Family reunions are celebrations that include multiple generations. Grandparents, parents, children, aunts, and uncles gather together. The past is remembered, the present is enjoyed, and the future is applauded. Church planting denominations have the spirit of a family reunion.

In a planting movement, it is easy to sacrifice the past on the altar of the future. But church parenting should never be seen as an either/or goal—*either* starting new churches *or* strengthening existing ones. Young churches need established churches to provide insight, resources, and a connection to the past. Older churches need new churches to provide vitality, refreshment, and a bridge to the future.

Denominational assemblies should feel like family reunions, gatherings of the extended church family that include and affirm all generations. By celebrating the past as the foundation for the future, denominations can further their rich heritage. Generations build unity by celebrating one another.

ALLOW FREEDOM OF EXPRESSION

Not so long ago, most people wore dress clothes to church. Wearing casual attire to worship was seen as a sign of disrespect. These days, blue jeans and sweaters are just as common in a worship service as suits and ties. True, some congregations prefer to dress more formally, but a healthy denomination allows for more than one fashion.

Just as styles of dress may change, ways of "doing church" may change also. The church has existed for centuries, but many congregations are finding new ways to relate the gospel to the culture around them. Those at the front edge of change are like the first people to wear blue jeans to church. Some may look askance at them, wanting to preserve the formality of the church—with *formality* meaning "church as we know it."

Creating a denominational environment that fosters church planting requires accepting various styles or expressions of the church. Those who prefer suits and ties will have to accept and appreciate those who wear shorts and sandals—and vice versa.

MAJOR ON THE MAJORS

John Maxwell originated the 101 percent principle, which holds that successful people find the 1 percent they can agree on and give it 100 percent of their effort.[3] Church planting denominations practice this. Because they are passionate about the cause, they refuse to fuss and feud over nonessential matters. They focus on the mutually agreed upon mission of "going and making disciples."

Are you helping your group to become a church planting denomination or association, one that provides both the foundation and flexibility for church multiplication? If not, why not?

SUSTAINING MOMENTUM

It begins with a subtle rumbling, a sense that something special is about to happen. A movement is gearing up; momentum is building. Usually, it begins with pastors and congregations who have a vision for multiplying churches. The movement spreads as church planters, districts, and other churches become involved. Soon, the ripple is spreading in all directions. That is the time when denominational and associational leaders need to act, providing the conditions that will sustain the movement's momentum.

How can they do that? What practical steps can a church leader or administrator take to harness the momentum generated by church planting?

KEEP PACE WITH LOCAL CHURCHES

First, denominations can encourage local leaders to drive the movement. A genuine movement will originate at the grassroots, the local church. Most often, local churches will set the pace, thereby forcing denominations and associations to adapt in order to keep up.

In Tacoma, Washington, a basset hound named Tattoo got his leash caught in the passenger door of its owner's car. Not realizing that the pooch was strapped to the side of his car, the owner pulled away from the curb and started down the road. A police officer noticed Tattoo's situation and waved the car over. The officer had clocked the dog moving as fast as twenty-five miles per hour. Tattoo was exhausted; basset hounds are not built for speed. If you could have asked Tattoo prior to this experience, "Can you run twenty-five miles per hour?" I am sure he would have responded, "No way! Look at this body; I could never run that fast."

But he did! Why? He had to!

When a multiplication movement takes off from the local church, denominational leaders may feel like a basset hound tied to a moving car. "Hold on!" they may think. "There's no way this structure can move fast enough to keep up." Yet they will be amazed to see how quickly the organization can adapt and change when it needs to keep pace with a genuine movement of the Holy Spirit.

NURTURE CHURCH PLANTERS

A multiplication movement will draw many people who are eager to get involved, including those desiring to start new churches. Some will be fresh from their ministerial training. Others will be called to join the movement as a second career. Few of them will have a sufficient base of experience or knowledge to begin planting immediately.

Denominations can serve the movement by providing an incubator to nurture potential church planters. The local church can give would-be planters ministry opportunities while the denomination connects them with mentors and provides training. Many of these future planters will operate bivocationally. This incubator approach will provide a nurturing, leadership-rich environment that prepares planters for their first assignment.

REDEFINE CHURCH

If a denomination is to embrace and bolster a church planting movement, it may need to redefine its concept of the church. Most denominations view a local church as a group of members that owns property and is organized into a certain structure with leaders, boards, and committees. That concept will have to be stretched for a denomination to foster a church planting movement. The term *church* will have to encompass house churches, cell churches, and other groupings that do not fit neatly into an organizational structure.

EMBRACE YOUNG LEADERS

Young leaders are the lifeblood of a church multiplication movement, and a denomination must embrace them if it will succeed in church planting. Emerging leaders are motivated by different goals than are older leaders. Those twenty-five years of age and younger generally have not embraced the Mega Dream: million-dollar buildings and hard-to-meet budgets do not fan the flame in their hearts. They want to impact the world with life-on-life ministry—ministry that is relational and meets personal needs. These young leaders form loyalties based on relationships rather than institutional structure and values. Denominations will have to adjust their thinking in order to create an environment for these leaders to thrive.

CREATE HYBRID MINISTRIES

Most organizations exist in order to perpetuate themselves. That is often true of denominations. There is a great deal of institutional momentum invested in preserving existing structures, and it is often difficult to respond to new needs. Denominations that foster a church parenting movement will break free from that mentality and become driven by a desire to meet the needs of people. Often, that results in the creation of *hybrid ministries*—ministries that do not fit easily into any existing structure or program. In order to create new ministries, denominations must learn to be fluid, adapting their structures to the current needs (rather than vice versa) and must accept the risk of failure.

EMPOWER, DON'T ENABLE

Empowerment is providing the resources for planting leaders to enact their unique God-given callings. *Enablement* is providing resources that force an unhealthy dependence on the organization. Money is not the key to success in church planting. Money should be viewed as a tool, not a panacea. Denominations can best foster a church planting movement by using it to empower planters who have demonstrated their ability to use it for the Kingdom.

STARTING NOW

Denominations play an essential role in the process of church multiplication. Local churches provide the energy and vision for starting new churches, but they need the support of a denomination or association. The sponsoring body provides the environment in which church parenting can take place.

Where does your denomination stand on the issue of church parenting? How effectively does it provide affirmation and support for church multiplication? These questions may help you decide.

- Do we, as a denomination, encourage church parenting? If so, how?

- What is the motivation for our church planting efforts?

- Do our financial investments reveal that planting is a priority?

- When we support church parenting financially, do we usually *empower* or *enable*?

- Do we have an adequate support structure for planters (assessing, training, and coaching)?

- By what means do we review the effectiveness of church planting efforts?

- What risks would we be willing to take to create a strategic plan for church multiplication?

- Do we have training opportunities in place for young leaders?

- Is this denomination willing to expand its definition of *church*?

- How flexible is the corporate culture in allowing local leaders to make decisions?

- Does our denomination view its role as planting churches, or as providing resources for church planting efforts?

Incredible opportunities lay before us. Denominational leaders can seize them if they are willing to break out of traditional molds. As church leaders work for change and begin to try new methods, there will be failures. But the denomination will grow in spite of those failures as leaders continue to learn, adapt where needed, and do what is necessary to create an environment in which Spirit-driven initiatives are encouraged.

May God give us the courage to take the whole gospel to the whole world.

CHAPTER THIRTEEN

SEVEN RIPPLE CHURCHES AND HOW THEY GREW

—⟋𝖂⟍—

> **RIPPLE PRINCIPLE**
> God continues to spread his gospel
> by multiplying churches.

I am an unabashed Starbucks guy. In fact, the majority of this book was written within the confines of a Starbucks coffee shop in Sacramento. Finding a Starbucks in my neighborhood isn't difficult. There are five of them within a three-mile radius of my house. Besides Starbucks, there are several other coffeehouses. In fact, two have opened for business in the past six months — within a mile of Starbucks.

If these were new churches instead of new coffee shops, worry would well up in the hearts of many church leaders. Discussions would be held around several questions. When is enough, enough? How many churches do we need in such a small area? Won't they water down one another's effectiveness?

Howard Schultz, the founder of Starbucks was asked whether the appearance of other coffee houses near his stores bothered him. His response was both revealing and liberating. Schultz observed that an increase in the number of coffeehouses simply raises the level of coffee consumption. As a result, all shops benefit. Incredible! In a day when market share is the driving force in many businesses, Starbucks has discovered that it's possible to thrive amid a crowded field. New shops are not competitors but comrades. Selling more coffee is the bottom line, and the more shops the better.

This is the attitude of the ripple church. The multiplication of churches in a given area does not pose a threat to any one of them. The presence of various kinds of churches actually raises the "consumption" of the gospel by touching more lives. Neighboring churches are not competitors but comrades. The bottom line is this: bringing people to a saving knowledge of Jesus Christ. When churches multiply, everyone benefits.

Interestingly, every Starbucks I have ever been in (and I lost count long ago) offers the same items. The coffee, the specialty beverages, the food items—they're identical in every location. What differs is the atmosphere. Each seems to have a slightly different décor and ambience. While I always enjoy the coffee, I do not always enjoy the atmosphere of a given Starbucks location. I frequent the ones that appeal to me most. In the same way, all Christ-centered churches offer the same gospel, but the atmosphere in which they offer it varies. The atmosphere provides a comfortable feeling and causes people to return to a particular church. Having a variety of churches in a given area will inevitably attract more people than any one church could.

RIPPLE MAKERS

Like Starbucks coffeehouses, ripple churches have popped up all over. They exist in all kinds of communities and share a common vision to create even more new churches. They are led by pastors who have a heart for people. These leaders know that many of the people around them will never be reached if they do not have a church that addresses their unique needs. Here are the stories of seven ripple churches, each one started to reach a given segment of its community. Together, they show that ripple making truly does make a difference for the Kingdom.

Midtown Community Church

Pastor Keith Klassen's ministry in Sacramento, California, was birthed by Arcade Wesleyan Church in the summer of 1998. Keith began this church with twelve people meeting in his living room. This small band of believers had a desire to be relevant to their community, build relationships with the unchurched, and multiply congregations. From this tiny handful, the church has grown to about seventy in number. It has moved from Keith's living room to a rented commercial space, and has already begun two house churches in different parts of the Sacramento area. This congregation sees multiplication as essential to meeting the diverse needs of the people in its region.

Spanish River Community Church

Under the leadership of Pastor David Nichols, this Presbyterian church in Boca Raton, Florida, has planted more than eighty churches—half of them located outside the United States. Spanish River runs approximately two thousand in weekly attendance. Some of the churches they have parented are Pointe Vedra Presbyterian Church in Point Vedra, Florida; Naperville Presbyterian Church in Naperville, Illinois; and Redeemer Presbyterian Church in New York City. The combined attendance of those three daughter churches is approximately 4,500 per week.

Spanish River plants churches that are expected to reproduce. Tim Keller, pastor of Redeemer Presbyterian says, "[Pastor David Nichols's] only non-negotiable was he wanted the churches to have a highly evangelistic vision. We've gone on to plant eight churches ourselves in the New York City area."[1]

Pastor Nichols did not always place such an aggressive emphasis on planting, but God brought him to this conclusion: "Church planting is one of the great loves of my life, all by God's grace. In the early days of Spanish River Church, I was busy with our own ministry and didn't have an interest in missions. But once I began to evaluate missions work, I concluded that the Lord's plan, as seen in the book of Acts, is that of building the Kingdom through church planting."[2] Large churches have the potential for large impact. The bigger the rock, the bigger the ripple.

CENTRAL CHURCH OF THE NAZARENE

This congregation in Tulsa, Oklahoma, was averaging 550 in worship attendance when it invested eighty people to begin Family Church of the Nazarene. On a recent Easter Sunday, the two churches had a combined attendance of over 1,200. A wonderful return is the result of a willing investment.

THE ROCK OF ROSEVILLE

Roseville, California, is a suburb of Sacramento and home of The Rock church. This is a nondenominational body of believers committed to expanding their reach through parenting churches. They began one congregation, The Rock of Granite Bay, in an adjacent community and are in the process of planting a second congregation in Rocklin, another adjacent community. One of The Rock's leaders told me that they have a vision to plant one hundred churches. Big visions call for a big God!

FIRST CHURCH OF THE NAZARENE

Pastor Joe Knight is a wonderful friend of mine. He led his Grand Rapids, Michigan, congregation in parenting two daughter churches in a nine-month period. During the parenting process, Joe recognized the need to refocus the mother church. The result was a new emphasis on reaching the growing international community in Grand Rapids. The parent church has renamed itself Grand Rapids International Fellowship and has a vital ministry to people of various races and religious heritages. Today the mother and both daughter churches are thriving. Parenting is a positive experience for the whole family.

MAGNOLIA WESLEYAN CHURCH

Poway is a growing community roughly fifteen miles north of Santee, California. Many years ago, the Pacific Southwest District of The Wesleyan Church attempted to plant a church in Poway, but failed. Pastor Frank Robinson knew that a church was needed there, however, and he led Magnolia Wesleyan in a daughtering effort. Magnolia, located in Santee, invested a staff member and several key families in the new church. Today, Amazing Faith Christian Fellowship is reaching Poway with the gospel of Jesus Christ. A local church can be effective where a district, denomination, or association may not be. When a local church takes ownership of a church planting project, there is a relational foundation not always seen in an organizational plant.

HOPE CHAPEL

Few have set the pace for church multiplication as Ralph Moore has. In 1971 he started a multiplication movement in Manhattan Beach, California, which has resulted in the creation of more than two hundred churches. Today Ralph is senior pastor at Hope Chapel in Kaneohe Bay, Hawaii, and the movement has spread to five continents. He observes, "As we struggle to grow individual congregations, the percentage of Christians within the general population is shrinking. . . . We need a new approach, because the old way only maintains the status quo, thereby diminishing the overall size and influence of the Church. *Aggressive church planting has the potential to reverse this trend.*"[3]

Moore hopes to see five hundred churches growing and reproducing by the time he retires. He calls parenting the "healthiest
agency for church planting."[4] Would the church he pastors be larger
if he chose to stop giving people away? Probably. But Ralph con-
cludes, "I would touch fewer people."[5] This is the heart of the ripple
church pastor. May his tribe increase.

This is a sampling of what has begun to happen around the country. God is calling local leaders, one by one, to parent reproducing
churches. The only factors that can limit this movement are our own
fears and unwillingness to trust God.

WHY NOT?

Karl Eastlack is the senior pastor of Eastern Hills Wesleyan
Church in Clarence, New York. He became pastor of this congregation in 1989. On his first Sunday, nineteen people attended. In 2002
Eastern Hills averaged more than 2,700 in weekly attendance. Today
God is leading the pastor and people to parent churches. Karl
explains: "I believe that it is time to 'ring the bell loudly' for a
renewed call and passion for birthing many more new churches all
across North America. Programming a movement will never work. It
must start with passion and sensitivity to God's heart for the lost
among us. It is happening around the world. . . . Why not here in
North America?"[6]

Indeed, why not?

Placed before us is an unprecedented opportunity. We have the
ability and the resources to launch a great church multiplication
movement. But it must begin at the grassroots level. Each of us must
catch the vision to take entire regions—not just communities—for
Christ. We must take God at his word, step out in faith, and expect
God to do something tremendous.

Every local church can do something in this effort. Some churches
can daughter new churches. Some can partner with other churches to
begin new congregations. Regardless of location, attendance, budget,

denominational affiliation, or organizational structure, every church can multiply!

I ask you to begin a journey that may make no sense from the church growth perspective. We have been trained to believe that bigger is always better. Yet I call on you to invest dollars, people, and energy into new congregations. It is a call to look beyond your own congregation and reach the souls who will never enter the doors of your church. It is a call to abandon old notions of achievement and success.

I believe the Spirit of God compels us to this. Yes, there is risk. Not every parenting effort will succeed; not every daughter church will survive. We risk our assets and our reputations to join this movement. The prospect may seem frightening. But God wants to breathe courage into our hearts. We must pray, as Moses did, "If your Presence does not go with us, do not send us up from here" (Exod. 33:15).

Every believer who reads this book owes a debt to another. It was because of someone else's vision, someone else's passion, someone else's willingness to risk that the gospel was preached in the city or town where you live. As a result of that sacrifice, you have a place to worship and to grow in the faith. By parenting new churches, you return the favor, extending the gospel for the sake of others. When you involve yourself in planting churches, you will touch the lives of a new generation of believers. People you will never meet will enter the Kingdom because of your sacrifice. I once heard Robert Schuller say, "Anyone can count the number of seeds in an apple, but only God can count the number of apples in a seed." Parenting a church is planting a seed. Only God knows what fruit will result.

And so I ask, are you ready to reach your world with the good news of Jesus Christ? Are you ready to extend your influence beyond your congregation into your community and across your region? Could you be the one who throws the rock that causes the ripple that makes the wave that changes the world?

Why not?

APPENDIX A

—◊◊◊—

ADOPTION MODEL MEETING

GUIDELINES FOR THE MEETING

- Set a definite beginning and ending time for the meeting.

- Have someone take notes.

- Clarify the purpose of the meeting. Participants need to know that a final decision will not be made at this meeting and that the purpose is to (1) discover the level of interest among this group in forming the core team for a new church and (2) determine whether an existing church will adopt this group and serve as a parent.

QUESTIONS

1. Is this group associated with a denomination, or do you all come from various denominations?

2. Why do you want to plant a church?

   - ❏ Disgruntled with churches in the area
   - ❏ Frustrated by the distance to your current church
   - ❏ Discouraged over the "traditional" church
   - ❏ Have a deep desire to see a community won for Christ
   - ❏ Other

3. What is your level of interest in planting a church?

❏ They are initiating the idea

❏ It is being initiated by the denomination

❏ The idea is mutually initiated

❏ Other

4. In your view, what does it take to start a new church?

5. What financial resources are at your disposal?

6. What kind of church do you envision?

7. When would you like to begin?

8. What is the average age of this group?

9. What life stage are most group members in?

10. Do you have any questions?

APPENDIX B

—ɯ—

CHURCH PLANTING CHANGE READINESS INDICATOR

	Yes	Somewhat	No
1. We have a conviction that the proposed change is God inspired.	3	2	1
2. The congregation has shown openness to change in the past.	3	2	1
3. Our leaders have a clear understanding of the present condition of the congregation.	3	2	1
4. Our leaders have a clear vision of where the church needs to go.	3	2	1
5. The leadership has begun to think strategically about the change.	3	2	1
6. We have identified potential problems.	3	2	1
7. We have identified key congregational leaders and made plans to bring them on board.	3	2	1

	Yes	Somewhat	No
8. Our leaders are aware of how to evaluate the change being made.	3	2	1
9. We have identified the congregational benefits of church parenting.	3	2	1
10. Our pastor is committed to the process.	3	2	1
11. We have communication systems to keep the congregation informed.	3	2	1
12. The majority of the congregation is under the age of forty.	3	2	1
13. The church has been in existence less than ten years.	3	2	1
14. No significant change has occurred in the church in the last two years.	3	2	1
15. The church has a manageable debt.	3	2	1

Points Possible: 45   **Total points** _____

The higher the point total, the more your church is prepared for change.

APPENDIX C

—⁓—

CHANGES EVALUATION TOOL

The CHANGES model for creating vision ownership (see chapter 8) can be invaluable for communicating your vision to the hearts and minds of others. These questions will help you apply the model to your church parenting situation.

CAST A VISION

1. Into what parts of the community or region can our congregation send people?

2. Who are the people that our church might reach through church parenting?

3. What is this church's vision of its future?

HAVE A DESIRED RESULT IN MIND

1. What models of parenting might best be implemented by this congregation?

2. How will we enact the value that we have for church parenting?

3. What might our region look like if a variety of new churches were started?

4. When do we envision this happening?

ADVANCE STRATEGICALLY

1. What church planting strategies have proven effective in our region?

2. What is the timeline for our plan?

3. What kind of team do we need to implement our plan?

4. What resources do we need to implement this plan?

5. What are critical milestones that we need to reach?

NEGOTIATE THE PROBLEMS

1. What five problems are we most likely to encounter?

2. Who might help us solve these problems?

3. What problem-solving resources are available?

4. How will we respond to unexpected difficulties?

GET THE CONGREGATION ON BOARD

1. What resources will we put into the hands of our leadership team?

2. What level of commitment should we ask of the congregation?

3. Who are the top ten people of influence that we must rally immediately?

4. What Scriptures will we use to build a biblical framework for parenting?

5. What hindrances, myths, and hurdles must be addressed in this congregation?

EVALUATE PROGRESS

1. What criteria will we use to evaluate progress?

2. Who will help us make regular evaluations?

3. What, if anything, would cause us to abandon this church parenting plan?

SHOW THE RESULTS

1. What benefits will our congregation enjoy as a parent church?

2. What benefits will our denomination or association reap from this effort?

3. What will we do to communicate these benefits to others?

APPENDIX D

—⟪⟫—

PLANTING TEAM MINISTRY DESCRIPTION

Responsible to: The pastor

Responsible for: Developing a workable plan to successfully parent a new church, which includes—

- Determining the best means of bringing the congregation on board
- Identifying people of influence in the church
- Deciding which parenting model will be used
- Developing a timeline from dream to deployment
- Writing a ministry description for the new church leader
- Clarifying expectations for the church plant
- Clarifying expectations of the parent church
- Developing of a budget
- Selecting the new church leader
- Creating a positive, uplifting commissioning service

Expectations: Team members are expected to—

- Be active members of the parent church
- Be committed to parenting a church
- Attend all scheduled task force meetings
- Become familiar with the planting process
- Read assigned books on church planting
- Pray for the parent church and the plant

APPENDIX E

—⟋⟍—

R ate yourself honestly in each of these thirteen areas on a scale of 1 to 5, 5 being the highest. If any of the areas do not apply to your experience, circle N/A.

Vision Capacity   1   2   3   4   5   N/A

- I have the ability to see what can be, not just what is.
- I can persuasively present my vision to others.

Intrinsic Motivation   1   2   3   4   5   N/A

- I am a self-starter.
- I am persistent in accomplishing tasks.

Ability to Create Ownership of Ministry   1   2   3   4   5   N/A

- I rally people to a sense of responsibility for a ministry.
- I am able to win the commitment of people to my vision.

Ability to Relate to the Unchurched   1   2   3   4   5   N/A

- I am comfortable around unchurched people.
- I understand the perspective of unchurched people.

Ability to Manage Family   1   2   3   4   5   N/A

- My spouse is supportive of church planting.
- I model wholesome family life.

Effectiveness at Building Relationships   1   2   3   4   5   N/A

- I make others feel secure and comfortable.
- I accept people where they are and lead them from there.

Commitment to Church Growth   1   2   3   4   5   N/A

- I accept steady and consistent growth without looking for quick fixes.
- I am committed to numerical growth, but not at the expense of spiritual growth.

Responsiveness to the Community   1   2   3   4   5   N/A

- I understand the culture of the community in which I am living.
- I have adapted a ministry to meet needs in a community.

Willingness to Use the Gifts of Others 1 2 3 4 5 N/A

- I know how to determine the gifts and talents of others.
- I match people's ministry with their giftedness.

Flexibility and Adaptability 1 2 3 4 5 N/A

- I can cope with change and flux in life and ministry.
- I can accept ambiguity.

Ability to Build a Cohesive
Church Body 1 2 3 4 5 N/A

- I include others into the life of the church quickly and effectively.
- I monitor the morale of others.

Resiliency and Determination 1 2 3 4 5 N/A

- I can ride the ups and downs of ministry.
- I have the ability to rebound from disappointment and discouragement.

Ability to Exercise Faith 1 2 3 4 5 N/A

- I believe in the power of God.
- I have attempted something based on the prompting of the Holy Spirit.

* Adapted from Charles R. Ridley, How to Select Church Planters: A Self-Study Inventory (Pasadena, Cal.: Fuller Evangelistic Association, 1988).

APPENDIX F

———✺———

SAMPLE CHURCH PLANTER COVENANT

I, _____, the planting pastor of _____ church make a covenant with _____ (parent church) and _____ (district/denomination/association) to

- Meet regularly with my coach and any other selected mentor
- Create a reproducing mind-set in the new church
- Parent a new church within three to five years of my launch
- Invest 10 percent of our church income back into the planting fund of my organization to support and sustain our church multiplication movement
- Participate in a support network of church planters
- Commit a minimum of five years to the new church
- Be loyal to my denomination and its appointed officials

Signed _____   Date _____
(Church Planter)

Signed _____   Date _____
(Parent Church Pastor)

Signed _____   Date _____
(District Supervisor)

Appendix G

—∿—

COMMISSIONING LITURGY

"Those who sow in tears will reap with songs of joy. He who goes out weeping, carrying seed to sow, will return with songs of joy, carrying sheaves with him" (Psalm 126:5–6).

Pastor: Today, we commission and release those whom God has called to expand his Kingdom through the planting of a reproducing church. As you go out from this place, do you commit yourselves to—

- Build a church pleasing to God?

- Share the gospel in word and action?

- Invest time, finances, and energy into [the community of the plant] and beyond?

- Grow through prayer and the study of God's Word?

- Continue Kingdom expansion through the planting of a reproducing church?

Core Team: We do.

Church Family: We, the people of [the parent church], called to invest beyond ourselves, release you with joy, love, blessings, and prayer. We will partner with you to reach our region and beyond for the glory of God.

Appendix H

—ᵐᵐ—

CORE TEAM COVENANT

As a member of the core team for _____
[name of new church], I commit myself to—

- Invest one year into this adventure

- Tithe my income

- Give above and beyond my tithe as needed

- Involve myself in ministry

- Pray regularly for the planter

- Invite unchurched friends and family

- Grow spiritually

- Be willing to stretch my faith to meet the unique needs of this endeavor

Signed _____ Date _____
(Core Team Member)

Please return this to the church planter.

APPENDIX I

—⁓—

BOOKS ON CHURCH MULTIPLICATION

Dillon, William P. *People Raising: A Practical Guide to Raising Support.* Chicago: Moody Press, 1993.

Faircloth, Samuel D. *Church Planting for Reproduction.* Grand Rapids, Mich.: Baker Book House, 1991.

Malphurs, Aubrey. *Planting Growing Churches for the Twenty-First Century: A Comprehensive Guide for New Churches and Those Desiring Renewal.* Grand Rapids, Mich.: Baker Book House, 1992.

Mannoia, Kevin. *Church Planting: The Next Generation.* Indianapolis, Ind.: Light and Life Press, 1994.

Moore, Ralph. *Starting a New Church.* Ventura, Calif.: Regal Books, 2002.

———. *Let Go of the Ring: The Hope Chapel Story.* Kaneohe, Hawaii: Straight Street Publications, 1993.

Sullivan, Bill M. *Churches Starting Churches.* Kansas City, Mo.: Nazarene Publishing House, 2001.

Schwarz, Christian A. *Natural Church Development: A Guide to Eight Essential Qualities of Healthy Churches.* Carol Stream, Ill.: ChurchSmart Resources, 1996.

Towns, Elmer L., and Douglas Porter. *Churches That Multiply: A Bible Study on Church Planting*. Kansas City, Mo.: Beacon Hill Press of Kansas City, 2003.

Wagner, C. Peter. *Church Planting for a Greater Harvest: A Comprehensive Guide*. Ventura, Calif.: Regal Books, 1990.

BOOKS ON LEADERSHIP

Blackaby, Henry T. and Claude V. King. *Experiencing God: Knowing and Doing the Will of God*. Nashville, Tenn.: LifeWay Press, 1990.

Easum, Bill. *Leadership on the Otherside*. Nashville, Tenn.: Abingdon Press, 2000.

Maxwell, John C. *The 21 Irrefutable Laws of Leadership*. Nashville, Tenn.: Thomas Nelson Publishers, 1998.

———. *The 17 Indisputable Laws of Teamwork*. Nashville, Tenn.: Thomas Nelson Publishers, 2001.

Sanders, J. Oswald. *Spiritual Leadership*. Chicago: Moody Press, 1967.

Stanley, Andy. *Visioneering*. Sisters, Or.: Multnomah Publishers, 1999.

VIDEOS

Logan, Robert and Steve Ogne. *Churches Planting Churches*. Carol Stream, Ill: ChurchSmart Resources.

Stevenson, Phil. *Mother Churches*. Order via e-mail: PStevenson@NewChurchSpecialties.org.

SEMINARS

New Church University, Parent Church Training, http://www.newchurchspecialties.org.

Dynamic Church Planting International, Daughter Church Conference, http://www.dcpi.org.

Church Multiplication Training Center, Bootcamp, http://www.cmtc.org.

NOTES

—〰—

CHAPTER 2: THE BIBLICAL ROOTS OF CHURCH PARENTING

1. Lou Holtz, *Winning Every Day: The Game Plan for Success* (New York: HarperBusiness, 1998), 107.

2. Jill Rosenfeld, "Down-Home Food, Cutting-Edge Business," *Fast Company* (April 2000): 56.

CHAPTER 3: THE MOST EFFECTIVE FORM OF EVANGELISM

1. C. Peter Wagner, *Church Planting for a Greater Harvest* (Ventura, Calif.: Regal Books, 1990), 11.

2. Oral presentation by Church Multiplication Training Center, Atlanta, Ga., January 1998 (http://www.cmtcmultiply.org).

3. Lyle Schaller, *44 Questions for Church Planters* (Nashville, Tenn.: Abingdon Press, 1991), 27–28.

CHAPTER 4: MODELS OF PARENTING

1. Al Goracke, "Good to Great," *Mandate Magazine* (Winter 2003): 13.

2. For more information on house churches, see Stephen Timmis, ed., *Multiplying Churches: Reaching Today's Community through Church Planting* (Ross-shire, Scotland: Christian Focus Publications, 2000).

CHAPTER 5: BARRIERS TO CHURCH PARENTING

1. Floyd Tidsworth Jr., *Life Cycle of a New Congregation* (Nashville, Tenn.: Broadman Press, 1992), 16.

2. For more information on Dynamic Church Planting International, visit http://www.dcpi.org.

CHAPTER 7: WHEN AND WHEN NOT TO PARENT

1. The material in this chapter is adapted from Phil Stevenson, "When Not to Parent," Church Health Fitness Center, October 2002 (http://www.wesleyan.org/ecg/fitness/parent_church_network/articles/When_Not_to_Parent.htm).

2. Two organizations provide training for refocusing: New Church Specialties (http://www.newchurchspecialties.org) and Church Resource Ministry (http://home.crmnet.org).

3. Church Health Survey using Natural Church Development Survey (http://www.newchurchspecialties.org/13-01-624.shtml).

CHAPTER 8: LEADING A CONGREGATION INTO PARENTING

1. This subject is treated extensively in chapter 10 and Appendix C. New Church University also provides training for developing and implementing parent church plans (http://www.newchurchspecialties.org/ncu.shtml).

2. John C. Maxwell and Jim Dornan, *Becoming a Person of Influence: How to Positively Impact the Lives of Others* (Nashville: Thomas Nelson Publishers, 1997), 146.

CHAPTER 9: FINANCING CHURCH PARENTING

1. Adapted from Phil Stevenson, "Preparing Financially to Parent," Church Health Fitness Center, April 2002 (http://www.wesleyan.org/ecg/fitness/parent_church_network/articles/preparing_financially_to_parent.htm).

2. An excellent reference for raising personal support is William P. Dillon's, *People Raising: A Practical Guide to Raising Support* (Chicago: Moody Press, 1993).

CHAPTER 10: BUILDING A PARENTING TEAM

* Training for developing parent church action plans is available through New Church Specialties (http://www.newchurchspecialties.org) and Dynamic Church Planting International, (http://www.dcpi.org).

CHAPTER 11: THE PLANTER AND HIS OR HER CORE TEAM

1. See Charles R. Ridley, *How to Select Church Planters: A Self-Study Inventory* (Pasadena, Calif.: Fuller Evangelistic Association, 1988).

2. The Wesleyan Church offers a Church Planter Assessment Center. For more information, visit http://www.churchfitness.org and click on "Church Planting."

3. Organizations providing church planting training are New Church Specialties (http://www.newchurchspecialties.org), Church Multiplication Training Center (http://www.cmtcmultiply.org), and Dynamic Church Planting International (http://www.dcpi.org).

CHAPTER 12: WORKING WITH A DENOMINATION

1. Bruce Feldman with John Gustafson, "Moving Mountains," *ESPN The Magazine* (March 31, 2003): 74.

2. Tim Chester, "Church Planting: A Theological Perspective," *Multiplying Churches* (Ross-shire, Scotland: Christian Focus Publications, 2000), 25.

3. John Maxwell, *People Power: Life's Little Lessons on Relationships* (Tulsa, Okla.: Honor Books, 1996), 35.

CHAPTER 13: SEVEN RIPPLE CHURCHES AND HOW THEY GREW

1. "The Art of Duplication," *Willow Creek Association News,* March/April, 2001.

2. Ibid., 6.

3. Ralph Moore, *Starting A New Church* (Ventura, Calif.: Regal Books, 2002), 21–22.

4. Ibid., 21–22.

5. Ibid., 53.

6. Karl Eastlack, "Super-sizing Your Church," *Mandate Magazine* (Winter 2003): 8.